White Ironstone

Stoltzfus, Dawn, 1972-
    White ironsrone : a survey or its many forms : undecorated, flow
blue, mulberry, copper lustre / Dawn Stoltzfus & Jeffrey Snyder.
        p.   cm.
    Includes bibliographical references
    ISBN 0-7643-0326-0 (paper)
    1. Ironstone china. 2. Stoneware--England. 3. Stoneware--United
States. I. Snyder, Jeffrey B. II. Title.
NK4367.I7S76   1997
738.3'09'42--dc21   97-20246
                                             CIP

Copyright © 1997 by Schiffer Publishing Ltd.

ISBN: 0-7643-0326-0
Printed in Hong Kong

Book Layout by: Blair Loughrey

Published by Schiffer Publishing Ltd.
4880 Lower Valley Road
Atglen, PA 19310
Phone: (610) 593-1777; Fax: (610) 593-2002
Please write for a free catalog.
This book may be purchased from the publisher.
Please include $3.95 for shipping.
Try your bookstore first.

We are interested in hearing from authors
with book ideas on related subjects.

White Ironstone

A Survey of its Many Forms

Undecorated
Flow Blue
Mulberry
Copper Lustre

Dawn Stoltzfus
&
Jeffrey Snyder

4880 Lower Valley Road, Atglen, PA 19310

to Andy

Acknowlegments

The authors would like to thank the collectors who opened up their homes to us in order to make this book possible and helped with the editing and pricing. These include Ernie and Bev Dieringer, Dan Overmeyer, Gale Frederick, Ellen Hill, and Dale Abrams. Thanks also go to Arnold Kowalsky for his willingness to help see the book through.

Contents

Introduction

White ironstone china came in many forms, body styles, and shapes. Many books have been written about the history of this ware and its shapes, but in this volume we will look at white ironstone from a new angle.

When we speak of white ironstone china, we are not merely referring to the plain white undecorated wares, but are also inexorably linked to many of the other fields of ceramics. Along with being manufactured undecorated, white ironstone also became a popular base, like an artist's canvas, for many of the decorations/treatments of its day. These include Flow Blue, Mulberry, and Gold and Copper Lustre (especially the seemingly ubiquitous Copper Lustre Tea Leaf and related motifs that were used). These decorated wares, along with the undecorated white ironstone, provide the focus for this survey of white ironstone and the variety of forms in which it may be found.

This book is intended to cross over different realms of ceramics. In these pages, you will be able to clearly view and compare what one body style looks like in plain white, and in other decorations. We will attempt to clear up some of the confusion between these different areas of collecting, and build on the common attributes of them all in order to provide new information useful for anyone interested in ceramics.

Displaying the wares of several different collecting fields based on their interconnecting relationship with white ironstone was a very difficult project to undertake. Each field has its own terminology. The authors are aware that because such terminology will not always jibe between fields, this first final result of such an attempt will be far from perfect. However, because such a book was desired by many collectors in different quarters, and because it can be very useful and informative to look at these interrelationships, we have made such an effort. We encourage others to pick up the torch and carry this project further.

When attempting to determine whether a shape or body style name was the work of a manufacturer or of collectors generations later, seek out registration and maker's marks and original registry drawings. If a name, given to a blank by a potter, is found in these sources there is no doubt it is the original. All other names have been applied to the wares in more recent times, and will be used in this book simply because there were no other alternatives and in hope of building a common language for collectors to use when discussing white ironstone.

White Ironstone China

by Bev and Ernie Dieringer

White Ironstone China, known as white granite in Staffordshire, England, has its roots in Chinese export ware and the inexpensive queens ware (creamware) and pearle white made in England during the end of the eighteenth and beginning of the nineteenth centuries. In 1813, Charles James Mason patented an improved china, harder than earthenware and stronger than porcelain, and called it "Mason's Patent Ironstone China". His patent lasted only fourteen years and by 1827 a number of other potters had experimented with similar formulas.

This early durable white ironstone had rounded, oval, rectangular, and panelled bodies. Some of the body styles showed an Asian influence, using plants and animals for handles and finials, while others had forms borrowed from silver and pewter services with their similar pedestals, handles, and finials often requiring six separate molds to make one covered tureen. White ironstone was decorated with transfer designs in combination with over and under glazed hand painting, Flow Blue transfer being the most common of these.

During the 1840s, some undecorated and cheaper to produce ironstone was shipped to the American market and met with great favor. Its demand was such that although it was cheaper to make, it sold at the same high price as Flow Blue, eventually replacing it in popularity after the middle of the nineteenth century. Competition and changing tastes required that new patterns be introduced to the market every few years. The earlier designs, with embossment only around the finials and handles, evolved into elaborate overall body embossment both in shallow and high relief. Every imaginable part of a plant—bark, stems, leaves, fruits, nuts, and flowers—were used in the embossing, as well as animals, shells, fish, and birds. These organic forms were well suited to the agricultural economy of the American market.

By the 1880s more than a hundred potters were producing embossed white ironstone. Many tons were shipped, and little can now be found in Britain. After 1870, white ironstone was also produced in America. Some of the potters were immigrants from Britain and brought their expertise to the industry. Towards the end of the nineteenth century the designs became simpler, returning to the plainer, geometric forms with little embossment. These round, oval, and rectangular bodies with utilitarian handles and plain finials free of decoration were the forerunners of all our early twentieth century mass-produced china found in schools, restaurants, hotels, hospitals, railroads, and in some ocean liners.

Ironstone china came in sets and special order pieces. There are dinner, tea, and chamber sets. Children's sets, which were exact copies of adult pieces, were also made. A dinner set included a large four piece soup tureen and a smaller chowder tureen, both of which came with a ladle and undertray. There were also several sauce tureens, smaller versions of the soup tureen, covered vegetable tureens in several sizes, platters in seven or more graduated sizes, open serving bowls, plates, and soup bowls in the same range of sizes used for everything from berries and honey to cereal, chowder, and soup. Relish dishes in imaginative shell and leaf shapes, some elaborately embossed with flowers, fruits, and buds, were also included in the set. Special order pieces could include a well and tree platter, a carafe, a reticulated fruit basket, a cheese keep, a compote with matching serving dishes, a punch or toddy bowl with matching cups, and anything else the Victorians could imagine using.

A tea set could include a teapot, a coffee pot, a large sugar bowl, a cream pitcher, cups and saucer (earlier cups had no handles), and a waste bowl for used tea leaves. Special order pieces could be a cookie plate, cake stand, and spoon warmer. The bath set would include a pitcher and wash bowl (sometimes called a ewer and basin), covered chamber pots of different sizes, a covered soap dish with liner, a covered horizontal toothbrush holder (sometimes referred to as a razor box), a shaving mug, and a small pitcher for scooping water. A master waste jar and a covered sponge bowl could be included. Footbaths and vase shaped toothbrush holders with undertrays were certainly special order items, since they are extremely rare.

Some of this collectible ironstone is being reproduced by museums and catalog companies. After 1950, an American company named Red-Cliff reproduced embossed white ironstone in a modern semi-vitreous ceramic. These reproductions were clearly marked.

There is an international club of collectors, The White Ironstone China Association, Inc., known as WICA. *White Ironstone Notes* is their quarterly newsletter. It features profiles of body shapes and portfolios of individual items in all patterns such as pitchers, tea pots, mugs, soup tureens, and compotes. Care and cleaning of ironstone and identification of marks,

and interviews of collectors and their collections are some of the other topics also covered. The Spare Parts column offers people an opportunity to find missing pieces and make marriages. The club's goal is to add to the study, history, and pleasure of collecting white ironstone china. For more information write:

WICA, Inc.
Box 536
Redding Ridge, CT 06876

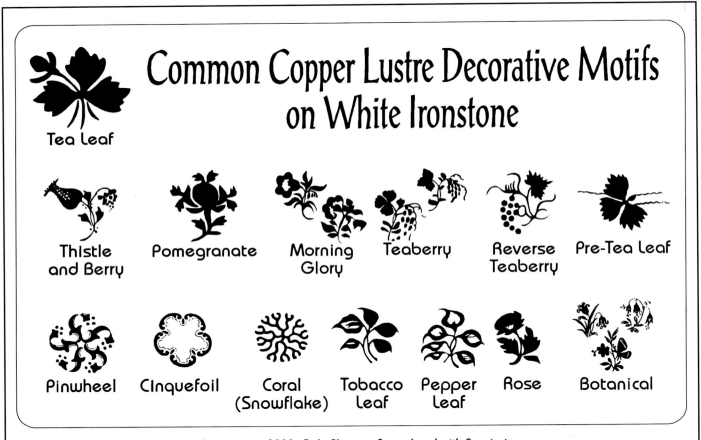

Common Copper Lustre Decorative Motifs on White Ironstone

Tea Leaf

Thistle and Berry

Pomegranate

Morning Glory

Teaberry

Reverse Teaberry

Pre-Tea Leaf

Pinwheel

Cinquefoil

Coral (Snowflake)

Tobacco Leaf

Pepper Leaf

Rose

Botanical

Drawings: c. 1988 - Dale Abrams - Reproduced with Permission
Copper Lustre Motifs article: c. 1996 - Dale Abrams
The Tea Leaf design is a registered trademark of the Tea Leaf Club International.

Tea Leaf Ironstone China

by Dale Abrams

Copper Lustre decorated ironstone china has a long tradition of popularity with the American consumer. When first produced in England in the mid-19th century, lustre enhanced ironstone, especially pieces embellished with the Tea Leaf design, was intended solely for export to the United States and Canada, where Tea Leaf became one of the most popular china patterns of all time. Tea Leaf and other copper lustre decorated ironstone has been used at American family tables for over 150 years.

What is lustre decorated white ironstone? Such pieces are normally characterized by thin copper or gold banding around the top and base rims of the pieces, lustre accents to handles and finials, and often one of the motifs pictured here is prominently added to the centers of flat and hollowware pieces. These copper lustre decorative motifs were applied to add variety and interest to the already-familiar undecorated white bodies.

The popularity of Tea Leaf prompted more than three dozen English potters to produce chinaware using this design, and another two dozen American potters to join in the craze later in the 19th century. By 1910, however, Tea Leaf production had waned. Although the 1960s saw a brief resurgence of Tea Leaf by Red Cliff (Hall China), an American decorating company, and Wm. Adams, an English pottery, the design didn't rekindle the passion it had held 100 years earlier. Today, however, collectors enthusiastically search for Tea Leaf to supplement pieces inherited from grandparents and great-grandparents. Today's collectors prize Tea Leaf and all of its variant motifs for its durability, simplicity, beauty, and style.

Anthony Shaw is credited with first introducing Tea Leaf, although other Staffordshire ironstone potters had used alternate copper lustre decorations as early as the 1840s. The number of potteries producing Tea Leaf, Teaberry, Morning Glory, and the other copper lustre designs accounts for the more than 115 body styles which we find lustre decorated. Of course, the English potters were in business to satisfy a wide range of consumer tastes and frequently the same body style was produced in plain white and also in a variety of other treatments including Flow Blue, Mulberry, Gaudy, Historical Blue, Copper Lustre, and others. This book only begins to scratch the surface of these fascinating interrelationships.

Tea Leaf Values

Tea Leaf prices vary dramatically and are intimately tied to several factors, including potter, body style, decorative motif, and condition. Because of the large number of potters and body styles, simple pieces like plates can range from $10 to $75 and up. Coffeepots are found for less than $200 and well over $500. As with all antiques, the collector *must* educate him or her self to be able to evaluate pieces offered for sale.

Tea Leaf Club International

The Tea Leaf Club International, founded in 1980, now has nearly 1,000 members in the United States and Canada and provides excellent educational material and social opportunities for its members. Through its newsletter, *Tea Leaf Readings*, and its wealth of educational publications, including the *Handbook of Tea Leaf Body Styles* referred to frequently in this book, the Tea Leaf Club is committed to education and member service. National conventions and regional meetings provide collectors with opportunites to buy/sell Tea Leaf and learn more about this fascinating field.

For more information about Tea Leaf, copper lustre decorated ironstone, or membership in the Tea Leaf Club, write to:

Dale Abrams
960 Bryden Road
Columbus, OH 43205

Flow Blue & Mulberry

The term Flow Blue describes ceramics which were decorated with underglaze transfer-printed patterns applied to hard, white bodied earthenwares; the ink forming these patterns was caused to bleed or "flow" into the undecorated portions of the earthenware vessel during the glaze firing. The desired "flow" was produced when lime or chloride of ammonia was added into the protective shell of the fire-clay sagger surrounding the wares during that glaze firing. Hand painted designs were also flown on occasion.

Flow Blue's softly flowing prints and durable dishes were popular in the American market from circa 1835 on into the first quarter of the twentieth century. Flow Blue table services, tea sets, and assorted crockery played their parts in Victorian homes, most significantly during dinner parties and teas.

The flowing color in Flow Blue, originally sneered at by British critics within the potting industry but nevertheless attractive and popular with overseas consumers, was also an aid to potters. Spreading over the white surface of their wares, the color bleed hid a myriad of potting imperfections from poorly joined seams on transfer prints requiring several sections to bubble in the body of the ware. This was wonderful for manufacturers as the Victorian ideal of the "perfect finish" was either great

realistic detail and meticulous surface finish *or* the concealment of the methods of production used to obtain the finished result. Flow Blue enabled manufacturers to meet the ideal with ease. In fact, some pieces were so heavily flown that the original pattern was completely obscured. As underglazing techniques improved, other colors were used to make flowing wares including mulberry, puce, and sepia, although blue remained the most popular.

Mulberry, also called "Flow Black", was a decorative treatment based on Flow Blue but which used manganese carbonate insead of cobalt to create a flowing purplish color. Mulberry was cheaper than Flow Blue, and was also a colorful alternative to the traditional blue and white pieces the public was used to seeing, which probably accounts for its popularity. Many of the same makers of Flow Blue were also making Mulberry in the 1830s-1870s, and often in the same patterns and shapes.

Ellen Hill, in her book *Mulberry Ironstone, Flow Blue's Best Kept Little Secret*, breaks down the over 400 patterns found in Mulberry into the basic groups of Asian, Brush Stroke, Floral, Marble, and Scenic. Consult this source for more information on makers, shapes, and patterns.

Makers' Marks

What follows is a pictorial guide to some of the manufaturers' marks found on pieces throughout this book. For more detailed infomation on these makers, see *Historic Flow Blue*, by Jeffrey B. Snyder. Unless otherwise indicated, the mark pictured was found on undecorated white ironstone. Please note that these marks have been dated using mainly Geoffrey Godden's *Encyclopaedia of British Pottery and Porcelain of British Pottery and Porcelain Marks*. These dates are an estimate only.

Adams, William & Son (s) Ltd. Tunstall and Stoke, Staffordshire, England. 1772-present.

Alcock, Henry & Co. (Ltd.) Cobridge, Staffordshire, England. 1861-1910.

(Copper Lustre) 1963+.

(Copper Lustre) 1963+.

1861-1880.

1861-1880.

Alcock, John. Cobridge, Staffordshire, England. 1853-1861.

Alcock, Samuel (Ltd.) Cobridge (ca. 1818-1853) and Hill Pottery, Burslem (ca. 1828-1859), Staffordshire, England.

1891-1900.

1853-1861.

1853-1861.

1830-1859.

American Crockery Co. 1876-. Trenton, New Jersey, U.S.A.

Barrow & Co. Longton, Staffordshire, England. 1853-1856.

Belle, J. & M. P. (& Co) (Ltd.) Glasgow, Scotland. 1842-1910 (23).

(Copper Lustre) 1876-.

1853-1856.

(Mulberry) 1850-1870.

Boote, T. &. R. (Ltd.) Burslem, Staffordshire, England. 1842-1906 (-1963).

1842+.

Bridgwood, Sampson & Son. Longton, Staffordshire, England. 1822-.

1853.

1890-1906.

ca. 1850s

Brunt, William Jr. & Co. East Liverpool, Ohio, U.S.A. ca. 1865-1878.

1865-1878.

Burgess, Henry. Burslem, Staffordshire, England. 1864-1892.

(Copper Lustre) 1864-1892.

Challinor, E. & C. Fenton, Staffordshire, England. 1862-1891.

1862-1891.

Clemenston Bros. (Ltd.). Hanley, Staffordshire, England. 1867-1916.

(Copper Lustre) 1867-1880.

1870+.

1870+.

Clementson, Joseph. Hanley, Staffordshire, England. 1839-1864.

(Mulberry) 1840s-1864.

Cork & Edge. Burslem, Staffordshire, England. 1846-1860.

1846-1860.

Davenport. Longport, Staffordshire, England. 1793-1887.

1852.

(Copper Lustre) 1880.

(Copper Lustre) Mid-19th century.

(Mulberry) 1820-1860.

17

East End Pottery (China) Co. East Liverpool, Ohio, U.S.A. 1894-1901.

(Copper Lustre) 1894-1901.

Edge, Malkin & Co. (Ltd.) Burslem, Staffordshire, England. 1870-1903.

(Copper Lustre) 1870-1903.

Edwards, James. Burslem, Staffordshire, England. 1841-1851.

(Copper Lustre) 1873-1903.

1841-1851.

Edwards, John (& Co.). Fenton and Longton, Staffordshire, England. 1847-1900.

1880-1900.

(Copper Lustre) 1880-1900.

Elsmore & Forster. Tunstall, Staffordshire, England. 1853-1871.

1853-1871.

1853-1871.

Furnival, Jacob & Co. Cobridge, Staffordshire, England. 1845-1870.

1845-1870.

1845-1870.

1845-1870.

Furnival, Thomas & Sons. Cobridge, Staffordshire, England. 1871-1890.

(Copper Lustre) 1871-1890.

(Copper Lustre) 1871-1890.

Gelson Bros. Hanley, Staffordshire, England. 1867-1876.

1869.

Goodwin, Joseph. (Probably J. Goodwin Stoddard & Co.) Longton, Staffordshire, England. 1898-1940.

1898-1940.

1898-1940.

Grindley, W. H. & Co. (Ltd.). Tunstall, Staffordshire, England. 1880-present.

(Copper Lustre) 1914-1925.

Harvey, C. & W. K. Longton, Staffordshire, England. 1835-1852.

1835-1852.

Holland & Green. Longton, Staffordshire, England. 1853-1882.

1854.

Homer Laughlin & Co. East Liverpool, Ohio, U.S.A. 1879-present.

(Copper Lustre) 1873+.

Johnson Bros. (Hanley) Ltd. Hanley and Tunstall (1899-1913), Staffordshire, England. 1883-present.

(Copper Lustre) 1883-1913.

Knowles, Taylor and Knowles & Co. East Liverpool, Ohio, U.S.A. 1870-1891.

1870-1891.

1870-1891.

(Copper Lustre) 1870-1891.

Mason, Charles James & George Miles. Lane Delph, Staffordshire, England. 1813-1826.

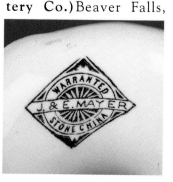

(Copper Lustre) 1870-1891.

(Note importer's stamp) 1820-1826.

Mayer & Elliot. Longport, Staffordshire, England. ca. 1858-1860.

1856.

Mayer, J. & E. (Mayer Pottery Co.) Beaver Falls, Pennsylvania, U. S. A. 1881-1964.

1881-1964.

1881-1964.

1881-1964.

Mayer, T. J. & J. Burslem, Staffordshire, England. 1842-1855.

1847.

1851-1855.

1842-1855.

(Mulberry) 1842-1855.

Meakin, Alfred (Ltd.). Tunstall, Staffordshire, England. 1851-1970+.

1875+.

(Copper Lustre) 1875-1897.

(Copper Lustre) 1891-1930.

Meigh, Charles & Son. Hanley, Staffordshire, England. 1850-1861.

1850-1861.

Meir, John & Son. Tunstall, Staffordshire, England. 1837-1897.

1863.

1837-1897.

Mellor, Taylor & Co. Burslem, Staffordshire, England. 1880-1904.

(Copper Lustre) 1880-1904.

Moses, John & Co. Trenton, New Jersey, U.S.A. 1863-.

1863+.

Pankhurst, J. W. & Co. Hanley, Staffordshire, England. 1850-1882.

1863+.

1850-1882.

1850-1882.

Phillips, George. Longport, Staffordshire, England. 1834-1848.

1834-1848.

Powell & Bishop. Hanley, Staffordshire, England. 1866-1878.

Red-Cliff (Hall China). East Liverpool, Ohio, U.S.A. 1957-1977.

(Copper Lustre) 1866-1878.

1903+.

1903+.

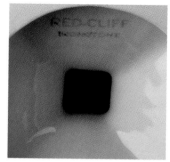

(Copper Lustre) 1903+.

Shaw, Anthony (& Sons) (& Co.) . Tunstall (1851-1858) and Burslem (1858-1900). 1851-1900.

(Copper Lustre) 1860-1882.

(Copper Lustre) 1851-1882.

(Copper Lustre) 1851-1882.

(Copper Lustre) 1882-1898.

(Copper Lustre) 1851-1882.

(Copper Lustre) 1851-1860.

(Copper Lustre) 1851-1882.

(Copper Lustre) 1860-1882.

Thomson, John (& Sons). Glasgow, Scotland. 1826-1888 (96).

Walker China Co. Bedford, Ohio, U.S.A. 1943-ca.1976.

(Copper Lustre) 1860-1882.

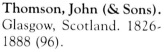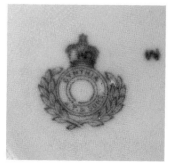

(Mulberry) 1866-1888.

(Copper Lustre) 1923-ca.1976.

21

Wedgwood & Co. (Ltd.)

Tunstall, Staffordshire, England. 1860-present. Ltd from1965.

1860+.

(Copper Lustre) 1860+.

(Copper Lustre) 1862+.

Wilkinson, Arthur J. (Ltd.).
Burslem, Staffordshire, England. 1885-present.

(Copper Lustre) 1885-1896.

(Copper Lustre) 1885-1896.

Wood, John Wedge.
Burslem (1841-44) and Tunstall (1845-1860), Staffordshire. 1841-1860. Note the confusion with this maker, who marked his pieces "Wedgwood", with maker Josiah Wedgwood; however, Josiah Wedgwood never marked his pieces with the initial "J".

1841-1860.

1841-1860.

1841-1860.

(Mulberry) 1849.

What follows is a survey of many of the shapes, forms, or body styles which were found in white ironstone, and some of the different decorations/treatments which were applied to them. In this book the treatments we focus on include Flow Blue, Mulberry, Copper Lustre Band/Tea Leaf, and some polychrome examples. Note that only those shapes *which the potters themselves named* use the term **Shape**, such as **Adriatic Shape** and **Asia Shape**. Shapes which were named by the maker but which did not includ the actual word "shape" are followed by "shape" in parentheses. (Example: **Tulip "Shape"**, which was named "Tulip" by the maker.) Shapes which have aquired names over the years, but were not named by the maker, do not have the word shape in their title, such as **Fishhook**.

In compiling the information presented here, the authors regularly referred to definitive books on each sub-ject; *White Ironstone: A Collector's Guide* by Jean Wetherbee, *Handbook of Tea Leaf Body Styles* by Nancy Upchurch, *Mulberry Ironstone: Flow Blue's Best Kept Little Secret* by Ellen Hill, and Geoffrey Godden's *Encyclopaedia of British Pottery and Porcelain Marks*. For congruity's sake, and in the hope of building upon her work, we have stuck to many of Jean Wetherbee's shape names, found in her books.

Listed under each shape name are the decorations/ treatments which a particular shape has been found in. Unless specified otherwise, it may be assumed that the shape can be found in undecorated, plain white ironstone. Also listed are the known manufacturers of each individual shape. This is not an attempt to catalog all possible manufacturers, but represents those manufacturers which are positively identified as having made a certain shape. Keep looking for new and rare pieces to add to this list!

Acanthus

This round shape, featuring embossed leaves, was made by the Johnson Bros. (Hanley) Ltd. and dates from about the 1880s-1890s. It is a similar shape to and is sometimes confused with Chelsea. Acanthus is also be found in Copper Lustre Tea Leaf.

Tea Leaf Acanthus plate, by Johnson Bros. 8 3/4" dia. *Courtesy of Dale Abrams.*

Acorn

Made by J. & G. Meakin, this shape has an acorn finial.

Adam's Scallop

Made by William Adams, ca. 1853.

Adriatic Shape

Made by Barrow & Co. ca. 1850s. A soft, rounded panel shape with a wheat/grain finial.

Alternate Loops

This round shape with alternating double and single loops was made by Bridgwood & Clarke, ca. 1850s-60s.

Arbor Vine

Made by Wedgwood & Co., a border design of vines.

Arcaded Double Ribs

Shape consisting of elongated ribs and arches.

Arcaded Panels

By John Venables, ca. 1850s, with panels and an elaborate leafy handle and spout on the teapot.

Arcaded Trumpet

Smooth arched shape with some foliage and a trumpet flower.

Arched Forget-me-Not

Circa 1860s, made by Elsmore & Forster, found with Copper Lustre treatments as well as in Mulberry and other transfer designs. Pattern consists of smooth panels topped by clusters of draped leafy foliage.

Arched Panels

General shape term covering pieces composed of well defined arched sides.

Arched Wheat

Made by R. Cochran & Co. (from Scotland), a border pattern of wheat and leaves, often with a pine cone finial. Found in Flow Blue and Copper Lustre.

Asia Shape

Made by G. Wooliscroft, similar to New York Shape. Arched panels around the bottom of the piece, foliage on handle and spout of teapots.

Athena Shape

J. Wetherbee found three pieces with an 1865 registry mark, but no maker. A border pattern of Roman-like designs and some foliage.

Athenia Shape

Made by J. T. Close & Co., registered 1866. Bands of decoration on pieces with a bar/cable-like finial.

Athens Shape

Registered by Podmore, Walker & Co. on February 23, 1857.

Fig/Union Shape (3 3/4" h., 3 1/2" dia.) mug shown with an Athens Shape mug (3 1/4" h., 3" dia.), both by Wedgwood & Co. *Courtesy of Ernie & Bev Dieringer.*

Atlantic Shape

There are three variations of this shape made by T. & R. Boote, registered from 1857-1858.

Atlantic Shape teapot by T. & R. Boote. 9 1/2" h. *Courtesy of Dan Overmeyer.*

Augusta Shape

Made by J. Clementson in the 1850s. This shape can be identified by its simple arched sides, found in Copper Lustre Teaberry and Copper Lustre Band, sometimes highlighted with Flow Blue.

Balanced Vine

Registered by the Clemenston Bros. in 1867, often found decorated in Copper Lustre Teaberry with multiple motifs on each decorated side.

Balanced Vine teapot by Clementson Bros. 9 1/4" h. *Courtesy of Ernie & Bev Dieringer.*

Ball and Stick

Made by James Edwards, ca. 1840s. Consists of long indents (sticks) with round indents at the top (balls).

Baltic Shape

Made by John Meir & Son, George Frederick Bowers, E. Challinor, and George Wooliscroft, ca. 1850s. Also found marked **Mississippi Shape** (E. Pearson) and **Maltese Shape** (E. Corn), this shape can be found in Mulberry.

Baltic Shape teapot in Mulberry *Dora* pattern by E. Challinor. 11" h. *Courtesy of Ellen R. Hill.*

Baltic Shape chamber pot by George Wooliscroft, ca. 1851. 7 1/2" h., 9" w. *Courtesy of Ernie & Bev Dieringer.*

Baltimore Shape

Made by Brougham and Mayer, ca. 1850s. Smooth panelled arched shape with little embossing.

Bamboo

Registered in 1873, manufactured by W. H. Grindley, Alfred Meakin, and John Edwards, this square shape takes its name from the bamboo-like handles and finials. This is a very common body style in Tea Leaf, and it is unlikely that it was made in undecorated white ironstone.

Alfred Meakin Bamboo sugar bowl in Tea Leaf. 6 3/4" h. *Courtesy of Dale Abrams.*

Alfred Meakin Bamboo Tea Leaf coffeepot. 8 3/4" h. *Courtesy of Dale Abrams.*

Alfred Meakin Bamboo Tea Leaf cake plate. 9" handle to handle. *Courtesy of Dale Abrams.*

Alfred Meakin Bamboo Tea Leaf relish dish. 8 1/2" w. *Courtesy of Dale Abrams.*

Alfred Meakin Bamboo covered vegetable dish in Tea Leaf. 4 3/4" h., 11" handle to handle. *Courtesy of Dale Abrams.*

Three piece covered soap dish in Bamboo Tea Leaf by W. H. Grindley & Co. 3 1/2" h. *Courtesy of Dale Abrams.*

Barred Wreath

A shape made by Henry Burgess ca. 1860s which is wrapped in a border of foliage.

Basketweave

Registered by Anthony Shaw, this square shape which features a basketweave-like embossing on the lower part of the body is very desirable. Basketweave can be found in Tea Leaf.

Anthony Shaw Basketweave coffeepot in Tea Leaf. 9" h. Courtesy of Dale Abrams.

Basketweave with Band

A variation on Shaw's **Basketweave**, this Alfred Meakin shape uses a similar basket-like motif with a diagonal floral band across the piece.

Beaded Band

Made ca. 1870s by the Clementson Bros. A simple round shape, found mostly in Copper Lustre Teaberry, which has a band of beads across the finial and handle which give it this name.

Beehive

An unmarked, round classical shape ca. 1840s found in several motifs, including Copper Lustre Pomegranate with leaves and sprigs.

Bell Tracery

Made by Holland & Green, this shape had a border of bells and leaves.

Bellflower

Two different body styles share this same name, coined by current-day collectors. One is John Edwards (Wetherbee, p. 199) and is similar to Lily-of-the-Valley by Anthony Shaw and other potters. The second is a Tea Leaf body style by W. & E. Corn, 1880s, which comes with a Gold Lustre Tea Leaf.

Berlin Inverted Diamond

This is a very unique and striking shape made by T. J. & J. Mayer, F. & R. Pratt, and T. Walker, ca. 1840s. This shape can be found decorated in Flow Blue and Mulberry, as well as plain white ironstone. Note that some Mulberry collectors refer to this shape as **Inverted Diamond Primary**.

Berlin Inverted Diamond teapots by T. J. & J. Mayer, in white ironstone and Brushstroke Flow Blue. 9" h. *Courtesy of Dan Overmeyer.*

Berlin Swirl

Registered by T. J. & J. Mayer, also produced by successors Mayer & Elliot, and Liddle, Elliot & Son.

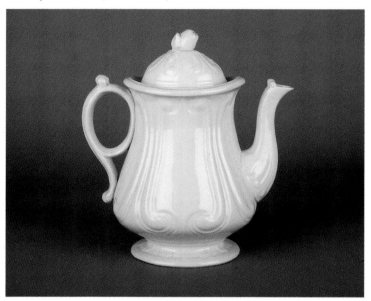

Berlin Swirl teapot by T. J. & J. Mayer. 10 1/2" h. *Courtesy of Dan Overmeyer.*

Vertical toothbrush holder in Berlin Swirl manufactured by T. J. & J. Mayer in 1856. 5 1/2" h., 2 1/2" dia. *Courtesy of Dan Overmeyer.*

Berry Cluster

Made by Jacob Furnival (J.F.) in the 1850s, this shape has a unique panel design of tall leaves and berries. Found in Copper Lustre Band and Teaberry.

Blanket Stitch (Piecrust)

This shape made by Henry Alcock and J. & G. Meakin, ca. 1880s-1890s, has "stitched" fluted bands found across the middle. Can be found in Tea Leaf.

Block Optic

Square body and handled shape, made by J. & G. Meakin.

Bluet

A floral design of raised lines made by Hope and Carter, ca. 1860s-1880s.

Boote 1851 Octagon

This was a very popular shape by T. & R. Boote, registered three times in that year.

Berry Cluster teapot by Jacob Furnival. 9" h. *Courtesy of Dan Overmeyer.*

Boote's 1851 Shape cups and saucers, one cup with a handle and one without. Cup with handle, 3 1/2" h., 4" dia.; saucer, 6" dia. Cup without handle, 3" h., saucer 5 3/4" dia. *Courtesy of Ernie & Bev Dieringer.*

Boote 1851 Octagon punch bowl and cups, with ladle. There are only two sets like this known to exist. Punch bowl 12" h., 10" w. *Courtesy of Dan Overmeyer.*

This Boote 1851 Octagon butter dish (5" h., 7 1/2" dia.), containing an inner plate, is shown with a pancake server (6" h., 9 1/2" dia.) of the same shape. *Courtesy of Ernie & Bev Dieringer.*

Boote 1851 Octagon shape gravy tureen with underplate and ladle. Gravy plate is 6 1/2" h., 6" w., underplate is 8" h., 6 1/2" w. *Courtesy of Ernie & Bev Dieringer.*

Boote Gothic

Rare **Classic Gothic**-style pieces made by T. & R. Boote.

Border of Leaves

Made by J. & G. Meakin, a border design of foliage.

Bordered Fuchsia

By Anthony Shaw, ca. 1865. This is the same shape as **Hanging Leaves** with the addition of Fuchsia leaves which give it its name. Note that this shape is so elaborate that there seems little room for the added Tea Leaf!

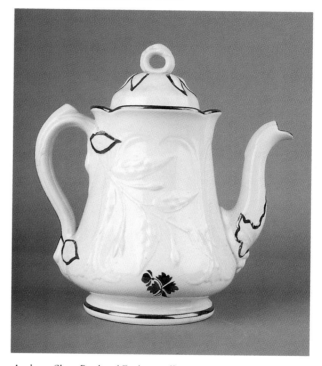

Anthony Shaw Bordered Fuchsia coffeepot in Tea Leaf. 10 1/2" h. *Courtesy of Dale Abrams.*

Anthony Shaw Bordered Fuchsia plate in Tea Leaf (9 1/2" dia.) with 4" cup plate and sauce dish. *Courtesy of Dale Abrams.*

Bordered Gooseberry

By Wedgwood & Co., once called "Branch of Three Leaves"(Wetherbee, p. 111). This is a similar style to **Flora "Shape"**.

Bordered Gooseberry pitcher by Wedgwood & Co. 12" h.
Courtesy of Ernie & Bev Dieringer.

Bordered Gothic

Made by T. Walker, John Alcock, Davenport, and Samuel Alcock. A Gothic shape with an added border and leaves on the finials.

Bordered Hyacinth (Lily Shape)

Made by W. Baker & Co. and W. & E. Corn, border design in leaves and flowers with a large flower finial.

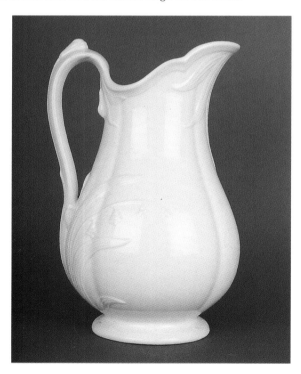

Bordered Hyacinth pitcher by W. Baker & Co. 13 3/4" h.
Courtesy of Ernie & Bev Dieringer.

Bow and Tassel

Round shape made by Burgess & Goddard (1878) with a rope-like circle and a tassel on handles.

Bow Knot

One shape was made by A. J. Wilkinson, ca. 1890s, and features a relief knot with one ribbon extending out of it on the handles of pieces, and can be found in Tea Leaf. Another similar shape by J. & G. Meakin has a simple bow shape on the borders.

Boxy Decagon

Made by John Alcock, ca. 1850s, the handle has some relief leaves and a split pod finial.

Britannia

Made by Anthony Shaw (registered 1878), this shape has a cluster of roses, shamrocks, and thistles representing England, Ireland, and Scotland. A similar shape is known to have been made by Powell & Bishop.

Brocade

Made by Alfred Meakin, ca. 1880s, this shape has leafy embossing around the base and finials. Can be found in Copper Lustre Tea Leaf, with no known examples in plain white.

Bulbous Octagon

Ellen Hill, our Mulberry expert, has identified and named this shape made in approximately 1845 by T. J. & J. Mayer. It is not known to be found in plain white ironstone.

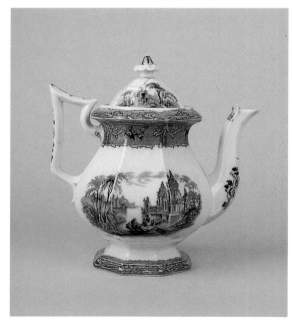

Bulbous Octagon in *Rhone Scenery* by T. J. & J. Mayer. 10 1/2" h.
Courtesy of Ellen R. Hill.

Budded Vine

This shape was made by J. & G. Meakin and impressed "1869". The rounded, all-over floral shape features the uplifted handles that would be popular in the following decade.

Bullet

This shape, made by Anthony Shaw, ca. 1880s, is only found in Copper Lustre Tea Leaf and features a bullet-like finial.

Cable Shape

This very popular shape was made in the 1870s and 1880s by J. & G. Meakin, John Maddock & Sons, Cockson & Chetwynd, William Adams, Henry Burgess, E. & C. Challinor, Thomas Furnival & Son, and Anthony Shaw. Some of the American makers of Cable Shape include Cook & Hancock and American Crockery Co. This shape is rumored to have been made to commemorate the laying of the Trans-Atlantic cable in 1866. A very popular shape in Copper and Gold Lustre, it can be found in Copper Lustre Tea Leaf and Pomegranate, and in Gold Lustre Cloverleaf and Morning Glory motifs. Some plain white ironstone collectors may refer to this shape as **Cable and Ring**.

Anthony Shaw Cable Shape coffeepot in Tea Leaf. 10" h. *Courtesy of Dale Abrams.*

Thomas Furnival & Sons Cable Shape pitcher. Note that this makers' Tea Leaf is a little unusual, it has an extra bud on it that the others don't. 12" h. *Courtesy of Dale Abrams.*

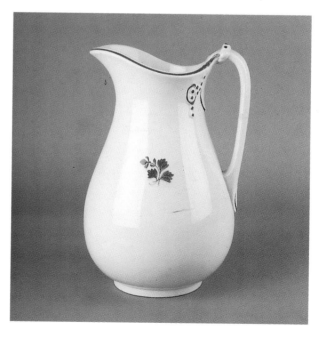

31

Anthony Shaw Cable Shape covered vegetable dish in Tea Leaf. 6 1/2" h., 11" handle to handle. *Courtesy of Dale Abrams.*

Anthony Shaw Cable Shape cream and sugar in Tea Leaf. Sugar 7 3/4" h., creamer 6 1/4" h. to lip. *Courtesy of Dale Abrams.*

Tea Leaf Cable Shape horizontal toothbrush holder or razor box by Henry Burgess. 9" w., 3 1/2"h. *Courtesy of Dale Abrams.*

Anthony Shaw Cable Shape shaving mug in Tea Leaf. 3 1/2" dia., 3 1/2" h. *Courtesy of Dale Abrams.*

Canada "Shape"

This rounded shape was registered in 1877 by Clementson Bros. It has a smooth series of arches around the base and a large embossed floral design of bluebell-like flowers extending across the body.

Cattail

Manufactured by Anthony Shaw in the 1890s, Cattail has a very unique finial marking which gives it its name. So far, the only identified piece we have found is in Copper Lustre Tea Leaf.

Brush box with the cattail handle which gives this shape its name, by Anthony Shaw. 8" w., 3" h. *Courtesy of Dale Abrams.*

Ceres Shape

This very popular shape was registered in 1859, originally manufactured by Elsmore & Forster, then Turner & Goddard & Co., Edward Pearson, James Wileman, and W. & E. Corn. This is similar to the **Wheat and Hops** patterns. It can be found in Copper Lustre decoration and Morning Glory.

Two Ceres Shape teapots by Elsmore & Forster, shown with a child's size version. Note that sometimes Elsmore & Forster put three different marks on Ceres, other times they did not mark their pieces at all. 11" h., 9 1/2" h. *Courtesy of Dan Overmeyer.*

Ceres Shape creamer by Elsmore and Forster, ca. 1859. 5 1/2" h. *Courtesy of Ernie & Bev Dieringer.*

Elsmore & Forster Ceres pitchers in Copper Lustre and white ironstone, shown with a child's teapot in the center. 7", 4 3/4", and 9" h. *Courtesy of Dale Abrams.*

Ceres Shape pedestalled fruit bowl by Elsmore & Forster. 10 1/4" dia, 5 1/2" h. *Courtesy of Dan Overmeyer.*

Ceres Shape pewter lidded pitcher. 6" h. at lip. *Courtesy of Dan Overmeyer.*

Ceres shape punch bowl with twelve cups by Elsmore & Forster. The bowl is 10 1/2" h., 10" dia; cups are 4" h., 3 3/4" dia. *Courtesy of Dan Overmeyer.*

Ceres Shape sauce tureen with ladle by Elsmore & Forster. This is the only sauce ladle that has been found in the Ceres Shape to date. 7" h. sauce, 8" handle to handle, 9" w. underplate. *Courtesy of Dan Overmeyer.*

Ceres shape egg cup, unmarked. *Courtesy of Dan Overmeyer.*

Ceres Shape pitcher and wash bowl by Elsmore and Forster, ca. 1863. The pitcher is 13" h., and the bowl is 13 1/2" dia. *Courtesy of Ernie & Bev Dieringer.*

Chain O'Tulips

Made by J. & G. Meakin, this is an embossed floral design with what looks like a ribbon, sometimes with a unique bow-like finial.

Chelsea

An oval shape made by Alfred Meakin, Johnson Bros., Powell & Bishop, and other American potters. Has a few panels on the sides with fairly ornate handles and finials. Found in Copper and Gold Lustre Tea Leaf.

Alfred Meakin Tea Leaf Chelsea platter. 14 1/4" w. *Courtesy of Dale Abrams.*

Chelsea relish dish by (Enoch) Wedgwood & Co. in Tea Leaf. 8 3/4" w. *Courtesy of Dale Abrams.*

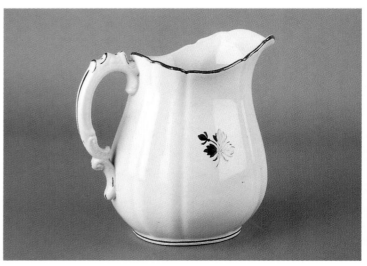

Alfred Meakin Chelsea style milk jug in Tea Leaf. 8" h. to lip. *Courtesy of Dale Abrams.*

Cherry Scroll

Jean Wetherbee has identified this shape by J. & G. Meakin. It has a border of scrolling designs and cherries.

Chinese Shape

First registered by Anthony Shaw in 1856, followed by T. & R. Boote (1858), J. Clementson, and Red Cliff in their 1960s reproductions. Rare shpae found with rosebud and pod finials, in Copper Lustre Tea Leaf and Teaberry and Gold Lustre Cloverleaf.

Anthony Shaw Chinese Shape coffeepot, sugar bowl, and creamer in Tea Leaf. The teapot is 10 1/2" h, cup and saucer 3 1/2" dia. *Courtesy of Dale Abrams.*

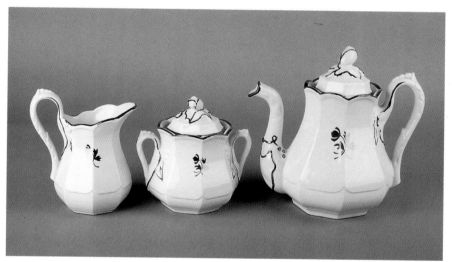

American Red Cliff Tea Leaf coffeepot, sugar, and creamer, a reproduction of Shaw's 1856 Chinese Shape. The teapot is 9 1/2" h. *Courtesy of Dale Abrams.*

Anthony Shaw Chinese Shape bath set in Tea Leaf. Pitcher (12 1/2" h.) and bowl (14" dia.), shaving mug (3" h., comes in three sizes), and chamber pot (9 1/2" h.). *Courtesy of Dale Abrams.*

Anthony Shaw Chinese Shape soup bowl in Tea Leaf. 9" dia. *Courtesy of Dale Abrams.*

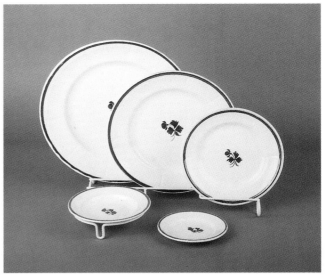

Anthony Shaw Chinese Shape plates in Tea Leaf. The cup plate is 4 3/8" dia., 5 1/4" sauce dish, 6 3/4" dia. plate, 9" dia. plate, and 10 1/2" dia. plate. *Courtesy of Dale Abrams.*

Anthony Shaw Chinese Shape sauce and soup tureens in Tea Leaf. The soup tureen has an Anthony Shaw imprint. Sauce is 7 3/4" h. and 9 1/2" handle to handle, soup is 13" h. and 14 1/2" handle to handle. *Courtesy of Dale Abrams.*

Anthony Shaw Chinese Shape covered vegetable and relish tray. The relish tray is 9" l., and the covered vegetable is 7" h. and 11 1/2" handle to handle. *Courtesy of Dale Abrams.*

Chinese Sydenham

This shape is an interesting combination of Sydenham and Chinese Shape, made by Anthony Shaw.

Chrysanthemum

Registered by Henry Burgess, this shape can be found in Copper and Gold Lustre Tea Leaf.

Citron Shape

Registered by J. Clementson, this shape has an embossed design of three leaves.

Classic Gothic

One of the early popular styles made in white ironstone by Samuel Alcock, Jacob Furnival, James Edwards, Livesley & Powell, Edward Walley, C. & W. K. Harvey, E. & C. Challinor, J. Clementson, Davenport et al., Mellor Venables, Morley, and Podmore Walker (watch for this maker's lion head cameos on the sides of their pieces) in the 1840s and 1850s and Red Cliff reproductions in the 1960s. Found in Mulberry, Flow Blue, Polychrome, and Copper Lustre Band, Pinwheel, Scallops, Teaberry, and Thistle and Berry . Included here are six- and eight-sided Classic Gothic. Also look for **Many Panelled Gothic** (ten or more sides), **Gothic Cameo**, and **Gothic Cameo Lion's Head**.

Henry Burgess Chrysanthemum vertical toothbrush holder in Tea Leaf. 5 1/2" h. *Courtesy of Dale Abrams.*

Classic Gothic shape teapots: the taller one is C. & W. K. Harvey and the smaller by Samuel Alcock. Harvey is 12 1/2" h., Alcock 9 1/4" h. *Courtesy of Dan Overmeyer.*

A great comparison shot showing many of the Copper Lustre motifs in the Classic Gothic shape. L-R: Lustre Band, Thistle & Berry, Pinwheel, and Teaberry (9 1/4" teapot). *Courtesy of Dale Abrams.*

Classic Gothic Mulberry
teapot in *Marble* by
Anthony Shaw. 9 1/2" h.
Courtesy of Ellen R. Hill.

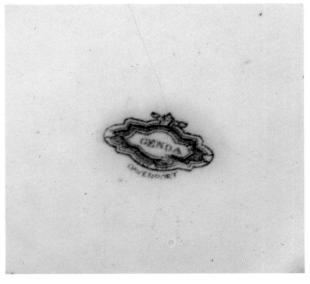

Classic Gothic Mulberry teapot in *Genoa* by Davenport. 9
1/2" h. *Courtesy of Ellen R. Hill.*

Classic Gothic Mulberry teapot in
Fruit Basket by F Morely & Co. 8 1/2"
h. *Courtesy of Ellen R. Hill.*

Six-sided Gothic teapot in *Fossiles* by J. Clementson. 8 1/2" h. *Courtesy of Ellen R. Hill.*

Six-sided Gothic shape teapot (sometimes referred to as **Lantern**) in Flow Blue Brush Stroke *Heath's Flower* by T. Heath. 10 3/4"h. *Courtesy of Gale Frederick and Dan Overmeyer.*

Davenport's Classic Gothic tea set in Flow Blue *Amoy.* 10 1/2" h. *Courtesy of Gale Frederick and Dan Overmeyer.*

Classic Gothic tea set in Copper Lustre Pinwheel. The teapot is 10" h.
Courtesy of Gale Frederick.

Another Classic Gothic tea set in Pinwheel, unmarked—possibly Furnival, a different manufacturer
than the previously shown set. This is basically the same shape as the above but the finials are different.
Teapot 9 1/4" h., sugar 8" h., creamer 4 3/4" h. to lip, pitcher 7" h. to lip. *Courtesy of Gale Frederick.*

Classic Gothic gravy boat with undertray in Mulberry *Peruvian*
by J. Wedge Wood. 4 3/4" h. *Courtesy of Ellen R. Hill.*

Six-sided Gothic pitcher in *Leipsic* by J. Clementson. 8" h.
Courtesy of Ellen R. Hill.

Classic Gothic pitcher and wash bowl by J. F. (Jacob Furnival). The wash bowl
is 12 3/4" dia., 6" h.; the pitcher is 11" h. *Courtesy of Ernie & Bev Dieringer.*

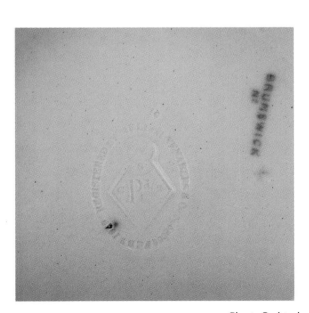

Classic Gothic three-piece sauce tureen in polychrome
Brunswick. 9" h., 9" handle to handle. *Courtesy of Ellen R. Hill.*

Classic Gothic sauce tureen by John Alcock. 7" h, 8 1/2" handle to handle; 8 1/2" handle to handle undertray. *Courtesy of Dan Overmeyer.*

Classic Gothic three piece polychrome sauce tureen in *Ava* by T. J. & J. Mayer. 8 1/2" h, 8 1/2" handle to handle. *Courtesy of Ellen R. Hill.*

Classic Gothic shape lidded pitcher by C. & W. K. Harvey, 6 1/2" h. *Courtesy of Dan Overmeyer.*

Classic Gothic eight-sided sauce tureen with under plate with generic ladle by T. J. & J. Mayer, ca. 1847. Note that T. J. & J. Mayer's pieces may be referred to separately as **Mayer's Classic Gothic**. Underplate 9" x 7 1/2", sauce tureen 7" h., 6 1/2" w. *Courtesy of Ernie & Bev Dieringer.*

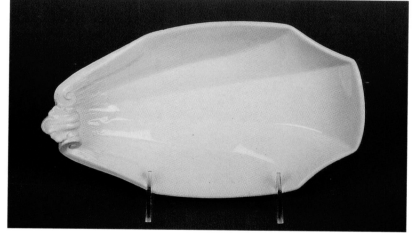

Classic Gothic relish dish by T. & J. Mayer, ca. 1847. 9" x 5 1/4" w. *Courtesy of Ernie & Bev Dieringer.*

Rhone Scenery Mulberry covered vegetable dish in Mayer's Classic Gothic. 7 1/2" h., 11 1/4" handle to handle. *Courtesy of Ellen R. Hill.*

Classic Shape

Smooth round shape registered and marked by T. & R. Boote in 1868.

Cochran's Ring

Shape with a border of flowers and leaves made by Robert Cochran (Glasgow, Scotland), named by Jean Wetherbee.

Cockscomb Handle

Circa 1840s, made by the Furnivals, Elsmore & Forster, Podmore Walker, T. Walker, this shape is rare and very collectible. Found in Copper Lustre Band and Teaberry as well as Mulberry and Flow Blue. The Cockscomb Handle pieces are not quite as rare in Mulberry and Flow Blue as they are in plain white ironstone and Copper Lustre motifs.

Cockscomb Handle tea set in Mulberry *Rose* pattern by Thomas Walker. Although the Cockscomb Handle is available in white ironstone, Flow Blue, and Copper Lustre Band and Teaberry, much more of it was made in Mulberry and so finding a piece in Mulberry is not so rare as it is for the other decorations. Teapot 9 3/4" h., sugar 9" h., creamer 6 1/2" h. *Courtesy of Ellen R. Hill.*

Cockscomb Handle teapot in Flow Blue *Morning Glory* and Gaudy *Berry* or *Strawberry*. 10"h. *Courtesy of Gale Frederick and Dan Overmeyer.*

Cockscomb Handle Copper Lustre Band coffeepot, unmarked. 10" h. *Courtesy of Dale Abrams.*

Cockscomb Handle creamer in polychrome *Phantasia.* An interesting pattern—the creamer illustrated in the pattern features a nude woman on the handle. Made by one of the Furnivals. 6" h. *Courtesy of Ellen R. Hill.*

Columbia Shape

Registered in 1855, this popular shape was manufactured by J. Clementson, Livesley and Powell, E. & C. Challinor, G. Wolliscroft, J. Meir & Son, Elsmore & Forster (on the Columbia shape the Forster name is misspelled as Foster), W. Adams, and Penman Brown & Co. The bottom half of this shape has embossed, shield-like panels similar to Sydenham. Found in Copper Lustre Band, Morning Glory, Tobacco Leaf, and Mulberry and Flow Blue.

Columbia Shape teapot in Mulberry *Rose* by Challinor. 10 1/2" h. *Courtesy of Ellen R. Hill.*

Cora Shape

A Sydenham variation made by John Alcock and identified by Jean Wetherbee.

Coral

A multi-panelled shape with a sea horse handle, made by John Wedge Wood (J. Wedgwood), ca. 1840s.

Coronet

Round shape with a crown-like finial made by W. & E. Corn, ca. 1880s. Found in Copper and Gold Lustre Tea Leaf.

Corn and Oats

Made by J. Wedge Wood, Edmund T. Wood, and Davenport, et al. The wonderful corn ear finial on this shape is what gives it its name.

Crabstock Dozen

Shape by James Edwards with crabstock handles and twelve panels.

Corn and Oats mug made by both Davenport and Wedgwood. 3 1/4" dia., 3 1/2" h. *Courtesy of Ernie & Bev Dieringer.*

Crewel

Made by Alfred Meakin, ca. 1880s-1890s. Named this because of the embossed patterns on the lower parts of pieces which resemble crewel embroidery. As far as we know, this shape is primarily found only in Tea Leaf or Copper Lustre Banded.

Crystal Shape

Plain rounded/bulbous shape made by Elsmore & Forster, ca. 1870s. This was made in Copper Lustre Morning Glory, Pepper Leaf, and Tobacco Leaf. Also named **Plain Scallop** by Jean Wetherbee.

Curved Gothic

Made by T. J. & J. Mayer and James Edwards.

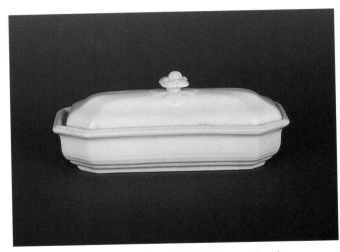

Curved Gothic horizontal toothbrush holder by James Edwards, ca. 1848. 7 3/4" w. x 3" h. *Courtesy of Ernie & Bev Dieringer.*

Curved Gothic/Long Octagon gravy boat and underplate with generic ladle by T. J. & J. Mayer, ca. 1847. *Courtesy of Ernie & Bev Dieringer.*

Daisy

Registered by Anthony Shaw, this shape has a daisy like pattern on its handles which give it this name. Found in Copper Lustre Tea Leaf, and not known to have been made in plain white ironstone.

Anthony Shaw Daisy gravy boat in Tea Leaf. 3 1/2" h., 8" w.

Daisy & Tulip

Made by Wedgwood & Co., 1880s-1890s, this round shape has daisies on the handles and finials. Found in Copper Lustre Tea Leaf only.

Daisy 'n' Chain

Squarish shape made by A. J. Wilkinson in the 1890s. This shape is found only decorated in Copper Lustre Tea Leaf.

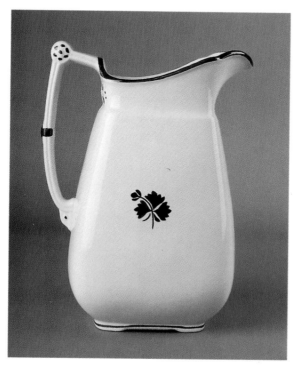

Daisy 'n' Chain pitcher in Tea Leaf by A. J. Wilkinson, ca. 1890s. 12" h. to lip. *Courtesy of Dale Abrams.*

Dallas Shape

A round shape similar to Sydenham made by J. Clementson, ca. 1850s. It is found in Copper Lustre Band decoration and has not yet been found in undecorated white ironstone.

Dangling Tulip

Registered by E. Pearson, in 1854, a multi-panelled shape with a floral design falling down from the handle. Also found with Copper Lustre Bands, but it is unusual.

Davenport's Squat Pot

Unusual oval shape registered by Davenport in 1853.

DeSoto Shape

Registered by Thomas Hughes in 1855, also made by Anthony Shaw. Found in Copper Lustre Tea Leaf and white ironstone.

Anthony Shaw DeSoto relish dish in Tea Leaf. 8 3/4" w. *Courtesy of Dale Abrams.*

Divided Gothic

A Gothic shape which is split line in the middle, made by John Alcock.

Double Line Primary *(see Primary)*

Double Sydenham *(see Wrapped Sydenham)*

Dominion

A very unusual shape registered by William Baker & Co. in 1877, with water lily handles and a beaver for the finial.

Dover Shape

Registered by W. Adams in 1862, this shape is made of long, thin ribs and leafy borders.

Draped Leaf/Draped Leaf with Berries

Four similar patterns have been named this, made by W. Baker & Co. (circa 1870s-1880s), James Edwards & Son (1859), Henry Alcock, and Bridgwood and Clarke. These are identified by Jean Wetherbee in *White Ironstone: A Collector's Guide*. This shape is also found in Copper Lustre Morning Glory.

Eagle (Diamond Thumbprint)

Made by the Gelson Bros. from 1867-1876. The finial is made in the shape of two eagle heads with their beaks touching; on some pieces the embossing is not so detailed which causes the shape to look like a diamond.

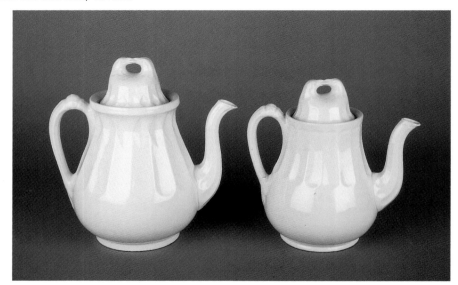 

Eagle (Diamond Thumbprint) teapots by Gelson Bros. Note the difference in the diamonds on the two pots. 9 1/2" h. and 11" h. *Courtesy of Dan Overmeyer.*

Eagle (Diamond Thumbprint) butter dish by Gelson Bros. 5" h., 6 3/8" dia. *Courtesy of Dan Overmeyer.*

Eagle (Diamond Thumbprint) sauce tureen by Gelson Bros. with undertray. Undertray 8 1/2" w., tureen 9" w. at handles, 5 1/2" h., ladle 7 1/2" l. *Courtesy of Dan Overmeyer.*

Eagle (Diamond Thumbprint) shape covered vegetable dish, Gelson Bros, Hanley, patent date 1869. Impressed "Patented 9 November 1869". 6 1/2" h., 12" handle to handle *Courtesy of Dan Overmeyer.*

Early Cameo *(see Gothic Cameo)*

Early Swirl

Registered by Frances Morley in 1845, this unusual shape has a few panels on the sides and an elaborate, embossed handle.

Elegance

A round shape registered by Clementson Bros. which has swirling, vine/leaf-like embossing at the handles and finial. Found in Copper Lustre Teaberry, not known to have been made in plain white.

Embroidered Chelsea

Oval style based on Chelsea (with added "embroidered" embossing), registered in 1884 by Henry Burgess. Found in Copper Lustre Band and Tea Leaf.

Empress Shape

Made by William Adams & Sons., ca. 1950s and 1960s. This is a 20th century shape (not a reproduction) made by the Adams company during the "Tea Leaf revival" (*Handbook of Tea Leaf Body Styles*), and found in undecorated white and with other decorative treatments.

Tea Leaf egg cups by William Adams in Empress shape. 3 3/4" h., 2" dia. *Courtesy of Dale Abrams.*

51

Tea Leaf coffee and teapots by William Adams in the Empress Shape. Coffee pot 9 1/2" h., teapot 6 3/4" h. These pieces were frequently marked "Micratex"—possibly a 1960s "high-tech" reference meaning they were dishwasher-safe. *Courtesy of Dale Abrams.*

Tea Leaf salt and pepper shaker set by William Adams in Empress Shape, also with Adams ceramic plaque. These pieces are unusual, Tea Leaf salt and peppers were not made during the 19th century years of manufacture, they are solely 20th century pieces. Salt and pepper shakers 4 1/4" h. Plaque 6 3/8" w. *Courtesy of Dale Abrams.*

Erie Shape

Made by Wedgwood & Co., ca. 1850s-1860s. A plain, round shape.

Fanfare

Made by Elsmore & Forster, ca. 1860s. This rather plain shape is often found decorated with Copper Lustre Tobacco Leaf.

Favorite

A very popular shape registered by W. H. Grindley & Co., decorated in Tea Leaf and many colored transfer patterns, hence the name "Favorite" (*Handbook of Tea Leaf Body Styles*).

Fanfare Tobacco Leaf covered vegetable (6 3/4" h., 11" handle to handle) shown with a Pepper Leaf relish, Crystal Shape (9" w). *Courtesy of Dale Abrams.*

W. H. Grindley Favorite coffeepot in Tea Leaf. 9"h. *Courtesy of Dale Abrams.*

Fenton Shape

Mason, John Wedge Wood, E. & C. Challinor, Davenport, and W. Baker & Co. are some of the potters who manufactured this shape, probably beginning around the 1840s. The shape is supposed to have been named by Mason himself (Wetherbee p. 204).

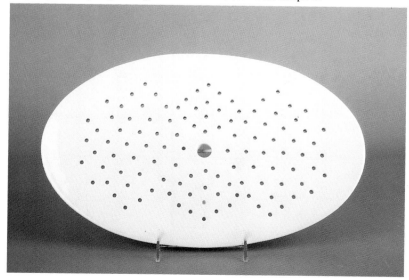

Drainer by E. & C. Challinor, Fenton Shape. 14 1/4" x 9 1/4". *Courtesy of Dan Overmeyer.*

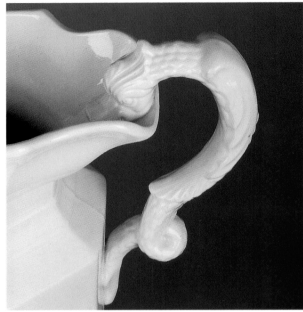

Fenton Shape pitcher with a dragon handle, which was made by both Davenport and Wedgwood in three graduated sizes. 8 1/2" h. *Courtesy of Ernie & Bev Dieringer.*

Fern

Round body made by J. & G. Meakin, features an elaborate fern handle and a central oval fern embossing in the center of the piece.

Fig "Shape"/Union Shape

Registered in 1856 by Davenport. Davenport and J. Wedgwood (Wedge Wood) both made Fig and Fig Cousin in the 1850s.

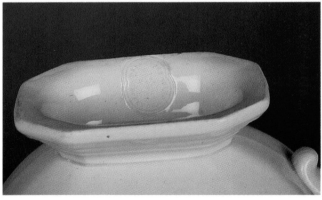

Fig/Union Shape gravy boat by Davenport, ca. 1856. 4" h., 9" w. *Courtesy of Ernie & Bev Dieringer.*

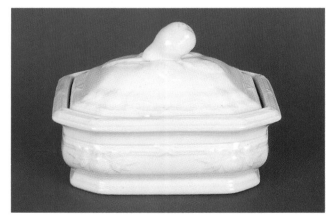

Fig/Union Shape covered soap box by J. Wedgwood, ca. 1850s. 4" h. x 5 1/2" x 4". *Courtesy of Ernie & Bev Dieringer.*

Fig Cousin

Registered in the 1850s by Davenport, found in Tea Leaf with Pink Lustre. A very collectible shape in Tea Leaf.

Davenport Fig Cousin creamer (6 1/2" h.) and sugar bowl (7 1/2" h.) in Tea Leaf. *Courtesy of Dale Abrams.*

Davenport Fig Cousin adult sized coffeepot in Tea Leaf shown with its child's size equivalent. *Courtesy of Dale Abrams.*

Davenport Fig Cousin coffeepot in Tea Leaf. 10" h. *Courtesy of Dale Abrams.*

Davenport Fig Cousin veritcal toothbrush holder with undertray, 5"h. *Courtesy of Dale Abrams.*

Fishhook

Made in the 1880s by Alfred Meakin. Along with Bamboo, Fishhook is one of the most common shapes found in Tea Leaf. The "fishhooks" can be easily seen in the copper lustre decoration on the handles. Of all the Tea Leaf available, this is perhaps the most plentiful.

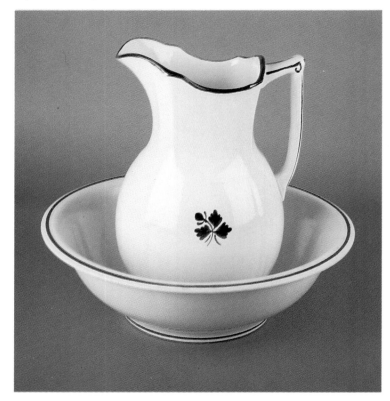

Alfred Meakin Fishhook pitcher and bowl in Tea Leaf. 12" h. pitcher to lip, 14 3/4" dia. bowl. *Courtesy of Dale Abrams.*

Alfred Meakin Tea Leaf Fishhook veritcal toothbrush holder. 5" h. *Courtesy of Dale Abrams.*

Fishhook sugar and creamer by Alfred Meakin in Tea Leaf. 7" h. sugar,
creamer 5 1/4" h. to lip. These come in many sizes. *Courtesy of Dale Abrams.*

Alfred Meakin Fishhook sauce dish and butter pat in Tea Leaf.
4 1/4" w. sauce, 2 7/8" w. butter. *Courtesy of Dale Abrams.*

Alfred Meakin Fishhook covered butter dish in Tea Leaf. 4 1/2" h.
The insert upon which the butter sat in the covered dish is shown off
to the right. *Courtesy of Dale Abrams.*

Alfred Meakin four-piece Tea Leaf Fishhook sauce
tureen. 7 1/4" w., 4 3/4" h. handle to handle. *Courtesy of
Dale Abrams.*

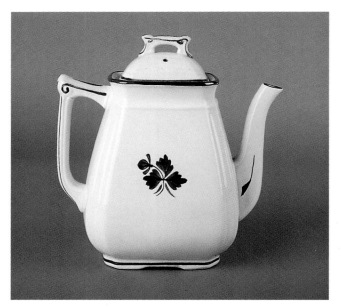

Fishhook coffeepot by Alfred Meakin. This piece can be found in many different sizes. 8 3/4" h. *Courtesy of Dale Abrams.*

Alfred Meakin Fishhook cake plate in Tea Leaf. 10" w. handle to handle. *Courtesy of Dale Abrams.*

Alfred Meakin Fishhook gravy boat in Tea Leaf. 7 3/4" w. 3" h. to lip. *Courtesy of Dale Abrams.*

Fleur-de-lis Chain

Wedgwood & Co. ca. 1890s, a shape featuring a ring of fleur-de-lis around the piece. Found only in Tea Leaf.

Fleur-de-lis with Leaves

Jean Wetherbee identifies this shape, by J. W. Pankhurst, which has large leaves and fleur-de-lis flowers around the sides and handles of pieces.

Fleur-de-lys

Registered by Mellor Taylor & Co., this oval shape found in Copper Lustre Tea Leaf (not known to have been made in plain white) has a unique fleur-de-lis finial which hints of royalty. When identifying this shape, Nancy Upchurch chose the French spelling due to the piece's "royal" style (*Handbook of Tea Leaf Body Styles*).

Flora "Shape"

Made by Wedgwood & Co., shape featuring a border of floral motifs.

Flora Shape

Registered by John Alcock, features a border of long leaves with hanging flowers.

Florentine "Shape"

Registered in 1850 by C. & W. K. Harvey. This elongated shape consists of eight panels and ribs.

Flower Garden Border

Made ca. 1880s-1890s by W. H. Grindley, this shape has an ornate border of several different flowers and leaves.

Flowered Hexagon

Registered by James Edwards in 1851, very similar to his other shape **Twin Leaves Hexagon**. Features a nice embossed floral handle.

Flowering Vine

An unmarked shape which has a vine with flowers extending around the borders of pieces.

Fluted Band

Made by J. Wedgwood (Wedge Wood), this shape is found in Flow Blue and Mulberry, and has sixteen long full panels divided by a band. This shape also may be called **Sixteen-sided Full-Panelled Gothic**.

The same two teapots, shown along with the sugar, and creamer in Fluted Band (Sixteen-sided Full-Panelled Gothic) in *Peruvian*. Sugar 8" h., creamer 5" h. *Courtesy of Ellen R. Hill.*

Fluted Band teapot by J. Wedge Wood. 8 1/2" h. *Courtesy of Dan Overmeyer.*

Peruvian Mulberry pattern coffee pot and two sizes of teapots in Fluted Band (Sixteen-sided Full-Panelled Gothic) made by J. Wedge Wood. The coffee pot is 11 1/2" h. and the teapots are 10" and 8 1/2" h. This set confirms collector Ellen Hill's belief that it is extremely rare to find a coffee pot; what most people call coffee pots are actually the larger size of two teapots. This set proves that two sizes were often made. *Courtesy of Ellen R. Hill.*

Fluted Band (Sixteen-sided Full-Panelled Gothic) sugar and creamer in Flow Blue *Chapoo* by J. Wedge Wood, ca. 1850. 4 1/2" h. creamer, 7 1/2" h. sugar. *Courtesy of Lucille and Norman Bagdon.*

Two pitchers, also in the *Peruvian* pattern and Fluted Band shape. Note that one is lidded for hot beverages. 8 1/2" and 7" h. *Courtesy of Ellen R. Hill.*

Fluted Gothic

A Gothic style shape made by James Edwards, ca. 1850s.

Fluted Hills

An unmarked fluted shape.

Fluted Hops

Registered in 1853, this fluted shape was made by J. W. Pankhurst & Co.

Fluted Panels

A graceful fluted shape made by James Edwards.

Fluted Pearl

Divided fluted shape registered by Thomas Edwards and then by John Wedge Wood (1847).

Below:
Fluted Pearl teapot by John Wedge Wood, registered in 1847. 8 1/2" h. *Courtesy of Dan Overmeyer.*

Foo Dog

White ironstone's patented inventor, Charles James Mason (& Co.), made this shape which had a Chinese Foo Dog for a finial and boar's heads for handles. Very rare.

Very rare Foo Dog finial soup tureen lid, marked Mason's Patented Ironstone with an importer's mark. 12" w. *Courtesy of Dan Overmeyer.*

Footed Primary

Hexagon Primary shape, known to have been made by Frances Morley.

Forget-me-Not

Made by E. & C. Challinor, Henry Alcock, Taylor Bros., and Wood, Rathbone & Co. Groups of forget-me-not flowers on this shape give it its name.

Forget-me-Not toothbrush holder (sometimes called a razor box) by Henry Alcock. 9" h. x 3" w. *Courtesy of Ernie & Bev Dieringer.*

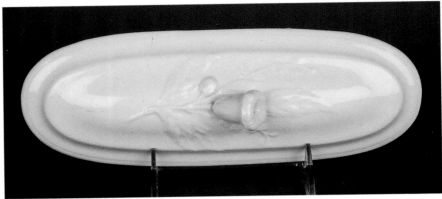

Detail of the Forget-me-Not toothbrush holder lid by Henry Alcock. Note that the finial is in the shape of a flower with leaves. 9 1/2" h., 3 1/2" w. *Courtesy of Ernie & Bev Dieringer.*

Four-Square Wheat

Square body made by R. Cochran & Co. (Scotland) draped in embossed wheat.

Fox and Grapes

Made ca. 1890s by Thomas Furnival & Sons, shape with handles of grapes, leaves, and a fox head.

Framed Classic

Classic hexagon shape made by James Edwards.

Framed Leaf

J. W. Pankhurst & Co. made this shape which featured eight panels with embossed leaves, ornate handles, and has been seen with both a split pod and an acorn finial.

Framed Panels

Shape identified by Jean Wetherbee, similar to **Six-Panelled Trumpet**.

Fruit of the Vine

Grape pattern made by J. & G. Meakin.

Fuchsia

Made by J. & G. Meakin and George Jones. This is a round shape covered in fuchsia-like flowers and leaves.

Fuchsia with Band

Made by Mellor, Taylor & Co., ca. 1880s and 1890s, this shape had a border of fuchsia with bands crossing over the leaves.

Full Ribbed

Entirely ribbed shape made by Sampson Bridgwood (Ltd.) & Son and J. W. Pankhurst in the 1860s. Found in Gold Lustre Cloverleaf and Gold Lustre Morning Glory.

Full Ribbed teapot by Pankhurst, 9" h. *Courtesy of Dan Overmeyer.*

Full-Panelled Gothic (Hexagonal and Octagonal)

Made by James Edwards, T. J. & J. Mayer, Wm. Adams & Son, J. & G. Alcock, J. Furnival & Co., R. Hall & Co., Podmore Walker, J. Clementson, Livesley & Powell, and Edward Walley. This **Classic Gothic** shape's panels go all the way to the bottom of the piece. This is a very popular shape in Mulberry and Flow Blue, and can also be found in Copper Lustre Band, Pinwheel, Teaberry, and Gold Lustre Morning Glory.

Full-Panelled Gothic teapot in the Mulberry *Castle Scenery* pattern by Jacob Furnival. 9 1/4" h. *Courtesy of Ellen R. Hill.*

Full-Panelled Gothic teapot in Mulberry *Moss & Sprig* (no marked maker or name) sheet pattern. 10 1/2". *Courtesy of Ellen R. Hill.*

Corean Mulberry Full-Panelled Gothic teapot. 8 1/2" h. *Courtesy of Ellen R. Hill.*

Full-Panelled Gothic teapot in Mulberry *Scinde* by Thomas Walker. 8" h. *Courtesy of Ellen R. Hill.*

Full-Panelled Gothic tea set in the Flow Blue *Shanghae* pattern by Furnival. Teapot 9 3/4" h. *Courtesy of Gale Frederick and Dan Overmeyer.*

Full-Panelled Gothic pewter lid pitcher. 7 1/2" h. at lip. *Courtesy of Dan Overmeyer.*

Full-Panelled Gothic teapot in Mulberry *Phantasia/Wreath.* 9 1/2" h. *Courtesy of Ellen R. Hill.*

Full-Panelled Gothic teapot in Mulberry *Chusan* by Peter Holcroft. 8 1/2" h. The spout on this piece was broken and has been soldered back on (an early innovative form of repair). *Courtesy of Ellen R. Hill.*

Full-Panelled Gothic Mulberry
teapot in *Lasso* by W. Bourne. 11 1/2"
h. *Courtesy of Ellen R. Hill.*

Full-Panelled Gothic Octagonal child's pitcher by James Edwards with
the full sized pitcher Full-Panelled Gothic Hexagonal by T. J. & J. Mayer.
3 1/4" and 8 7/8" h. to lip respectively. *Courtesy of Dan Overmeyer.*

Garden Sprig

Round shape by J. & G. Meakin covered in a group of flowers and foliage.

Garibaldi Shape

Registered in 1860 by T. & R. Boote, a round shape with a floral/leafy handle.

Garland

Border of ribbons and flowers made by Cockson, Chetwynd & Co.

Gentle Square (Rooster)

Registered in 1876 by Thomas Furnival & Sons and found in the Tea Leaf decoration. The name "rooster" comes from the handle which has a bird-head shape on either side.

Furnival & Son Gentle Square (Rooster) sugar bowl in Tea Leaf. 6 1/2" h. *Courtesy of Dale Abrams.*

T. Furnival & Son Gentle Square (Rooster) tray. 13 1/4" w. *Courtesy of Dale Abrams.*

Furnival & Sons covered butter in Gentle Square (Rooster) Tea Leaf. 4 1/4" h. *Courtesy of Dale Abrams.*

Girard Shape

Ocatagon shape made by J. Ridgway Bates & Co. (1856-1858), with panels and shields reminiscent of Sydenham, floral embossing on the handles and finials.

Golden Scroll

Made by Powell & Bishop and then Bishop and Stonier, ca. 1880s-1890s, named this because of the scrolled embossed designs on the pieces. Found in Gold Lustre Band and Gold Lustre Tea Leaf.

Gooseberry

Made by J. F. (Jacob Furnival), round shape with scalloped edges and large leafy designs around the handles.

Gothic "Shape" by Holland & Green

Holland & Green made their own Gothic Shape in ca. 1850s, with decorative embossed panels and shields, very different from the other shapes referred to as Classic Gothic or Gothic.

Gothic "Shape" teapot by Holland & Green, 1854. 10" h. *Courtesy of Dan Overmeyer.*

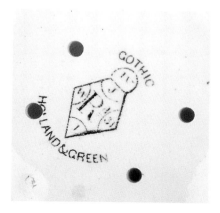

Gothic "Shape" brush holder with undertray by Holland & Green. 5 3/4" h. holder, 4 1/2" w. undertray (5" to points). *Courtesy of Dan Overmeyer.*

Gothic Cameo

Made by John Alcock, James Edwards, J. Wedge Wood, Davenport, and Edward Walley (who registered the shape in 1847). This eight-sided shape can be found in Copper Lustre Tea Leaf, Copper Lustre Band, Mulberry, and Flow Blue.

Gothic Cameo gravy boat in Mulberry *Vincennes* by Alcock. Note the face on the handle, the distinguishing feature which gives this shape its name. 6" h. *Courtesy of Ellen R. Hill.*

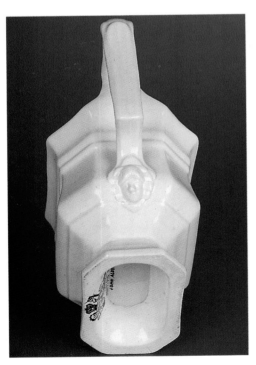 

Gothic Cameo gravy boat by John Alcock, ca. 1848.
7 1/2" l., 5" h. *Courtesy of Ernie & Bev Dieringer.*

Gothic Cameo relish dish by James
Edwards, ca. 1848. 9" x 4". *Courtesy of
Ernie & Bev Dieringer.*

Gothic Cameo fruit compote by John Alcock.
8 1/4" h., 10 1/2" w. *Courtesy of Ernie & Bev Dieringer.*

Gothic Cameo Lion's Head Handle

A version of **Gothic Cameo** which replaces a human head with a lion's on the handles, made by Podmore, Walker & Co. ca. 1840s. So far this shape has been seen only in Flow Blue.

Below:
Gothic Cameo Lion's Head Handle *Temple* tea set by Podmore, Walker & Co. 9" h. *Courtesy of Gale Frederick and Dan Overmeyer.*

Right:
Sugar bowl in Flow Blue *Geraneum* on the Gothic Cameo Lion's Head Handle shape. *Courtesy of Dorothy & Elmer Caskey, Trojan Antiques, Cynthiana, Kentucky 41031.*

Gothic Grape

Made by Jacob Furnvial, ca. 1850s, a **Classic Gothic** shape with a grape cluster finial.

Gothic Rose

Made by Charles Meigh & Son, another **Classic Gothic** shape with a rose bud and leaves for a finial.

Gourd

Round shape made by James Edwards & Son, ca. 1850s, with a large gourd finial.

Grand Loop

Made by Jacob Furnival (J. F.) in the 1860s, found in Copper Lustre Band, Cinquefoil, Botanicals, Teaberry, and Copper Lustre with Flow Blue (by Mellor, Venables & Company and others).

Grand Loop pieces in Lustre Band, Teaberry, and Blue Leaves with Red Pinstripes. *Courtesy of Dale Abrams.*

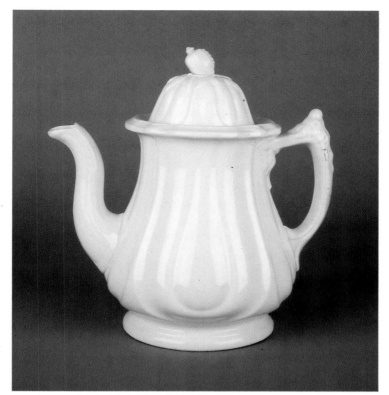

Grand Loop teapot by
Jacob Furnival. This teapot
can be found with two
different finials. 10 1/2" h.
Courtesy of Dan Overmeyer.

Grape Clusters

Large embossed grape design made by Davenport, ca. 1870s.

Grape Clusters with Chain

Similar to **Grape Clusters**, this shape made by Henry Burgess ca. 1870s also had a large embossed grape design, with the addition of a chain circling the shape.

Grape Octagon

Made mostly in the 1840s and 1850s. Jacob Furnival, E. Challinor & Co., J. Clementson, Elsmore & Forster, Bougham & Mayer, Lively & Powell, Edward Corn, Samuel Alcock, Thomas Walker, Hulme & Booth, Freakly & Farrell, Venables, Mann & Co., E. Hughes & Co., and Edward Walley were some of the potters who made versions of this very popular shape. Red Cliff, an American company, also decorated reproductions of Grape Octagon around the middle of the twentieth century. This shape can be found in Copper Lustre Band, Pinwheel, Pomegranate, Pre-Tea Leaf, Teaberry, and Thistle and Berry, as well as Flow Blue and Mulberry.

Grape Octagon covered vegetable dish in Pinwheel. 8" h.
Courtesy of Gale Frederick.

Grape Octagon covered vegetable dish in polychrome *Cotton Plant* by Jacob Furnival. 8" h., 9 1/2" w. *Courtesy of Ellen R. Hill.*

A good display of Grape Octagon Copper Lustre pieces, in
Lustre Band, Pinwheel, and Teaberry. *Courtesy of Dale Abrams.*

Grape Octagon covered vegetable and coffeepot in Copper Lustre
motifs Thistle and Berry and Pomegranate. *Courtesy of Dale Abrams.*

Grape Octagon fruit compote in Pinwheel. 8 1/2" h., 9 3/4" dia.
Courtesy of Gale Frederick.

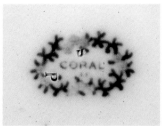

Grape Octagon gravy boat with undertray in Mulberry *Coral* by J. Furnival. 5". *Courtesy of Ellen R. Hill.*

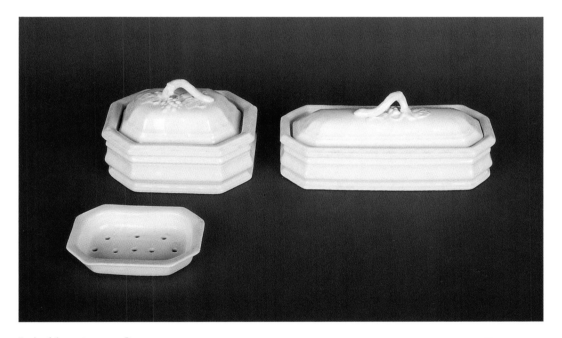

Both of these pieces are Grape Octagon, maker unknown. The covered soap box is 5 1/4" x 4" by 4" h. and the toothbrush holder is 7 1/4" x 3 1/4" 3 1/4" h. *Courtesy of Ernie & Bev Dieringer.*

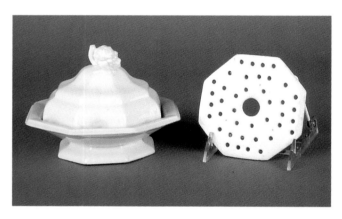

Grape Vine

Made by the Clementson Bros. ca. 1880s, round shape with a grape leaf and spiral handle and finials. As far as we know, this shape is only found in Copper Lustre Teaberry.

Grape Wreath

Made by Bridgwood & Clarke, this is a shape with a border pattern of winding vines and leaves with clusters of grapes.

Great Ivy with Berries

Made by John Maddock & Sons, ca. 1840s-1850s, featuring large embossed ivy leaves with berries.

Greek Key

Greco-Roman border design made by J. W. Pankhurst, registered in 1863.

Grenade Shape

Made by Henry Burgess ca. 1860s (in Copper Lustre Tea Leaf) and by T. & R. Boote (plain white ironstone), distinctive because of its groups of three leaves.

Halleck Shape (Morning Glory)

Made by Elsmore & Forster, ca. 1860s.

Halleck Shape (Morning Glory) mug by Elsmore & Forster, ca. 1860s. 4" dia., 3 3/4" h. *Courtesy of Ernie & Bev Dieringer.*

Hanging Arch

This shape, made by James Edwards & Son, is composed of arches and clusters of foliage.

Hanging Leaves

Bulbous shape made ca. 1850s-1860s, found in Tea Leaf.

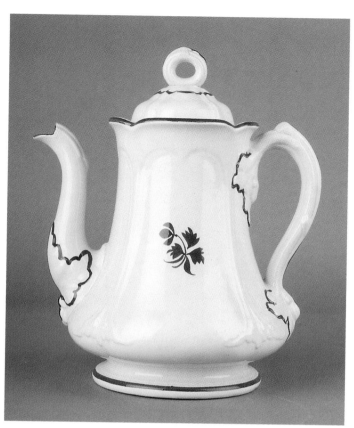

Anthony Shaw Hanging Leaves pitcher (7 1/2" h.), mug (4" h., 3 3/4" dia.), and sauce dish (5" dia.) in Tea Leaf. *Courtesy of Dale Abrams.*

Anthony Shaw Hanging Leaves coffeepot in Tea Leaf. 10 1/4" h. *Courtesy of Dale Abrams.*

Anthony Shaw Hanging Leaves soup plate in Tea Leaf. 9 3/4" dia. *Courtesy of Dale Abrams.*

Hanging Leaves brush box by Anthony Shaw in Tea Leaf. 9" w., 3 1/2" h. *Courtesy of Dale Abrams.*

Hanging Pear

Made by Liddle, Elliot & Son, this shape has an embossed pear with leaves hanging from a stalk.

Havelock Shape

Holland & Green ca. 1850s shape, made with a ring handle and finial, and raspberry and wheat decorations.

Haveloch shape teapot by Holland & Green, 1852. 11" h.
Courtesy of Dan Overmeyer.

Havre Shape

Plain shape, maker unknown.

Hawthorn

Made by A. J. Wilkinson, ca. 1880s-1890s. A round or oval shape with hawthorn leaves on the handles and finials. This shape is not known to have been made in plain white ironstone and has been found in Copper Lustre Tea Leaf only.

Hawthorne's Fern

Round shape registered on March 19, 1879 by John Hawthorne featuring a large embossed fern leaf.

Heavy Square

Registered by the Clementson Bros., this shape is found in Copper Lustre Teaberry and Tea Leaf and is not known have been made in plain white ironstone.

Hebe Shape

Shape with acorn and leaf finial registered by John Alcock in 1853.

Hexagon Strap

Made ca. late 1880s by Sampson Bridgwood & Son (Ltd.), bar handle and finial.

Hexagon Sunburst

Made by Anthony Shaw, ca. 1880s, named for its sunburst finials and handles. Found in Copper Lustre Tea Leaf (where it is referred to as simply **Hexagon**).

Hidden Motif

Named for its small floral motif, also decorated with larger embossed foliage. Made by Jacob Furnival & Co..

Hill Shape (Medallion Scroll)

Registered in 1860 by John Clementson, this shape is found in Copper Lustre Band, Coral, and Teaberry, and Blue and Copper.

Holly

Made by John Maddock & Son, ca. 1850s, this round shape has holly leaves on the spout and handle.

Huron Shape

A round shape with characteristic shields and arrowhead shapes registered by William Adams in 1858. Made in Tea Leaf.

Tea Leaf Heavy Square sugar bowl by the Clementson Bros. 7 1/4" h.
Courtesy of Dale Abrams.

Hill Shape Blue and Copper sugar bowl, 8 1/2" h.
Courtesy of Dale Abrams.

Hyacinth "Shape"

Made by Wedgwood & Co. and W. & E. Corn, this is a large embossed shape with leaves and flowers covering the entire piece.

Hyacinth

A slightly different Hyacinth, found in white ironstone by several potters and in the Copper Lustre Pre-Tea Leaf motif by R. Cochran & Co. (Scotland). This shape has a border of leaves and flowers.

Hydra "Shape"

White granite shape made in the 1830s by Charles Mason.

Hydra Hexagon

Classic Gothic shape, ca. 1840s, no known maker.

Iona "Shape" *(see Square Ridged: Iona)*

Ivy Wreath

Registered by J. Meir & Son in 1860, shape covered in heavy ivy leaves and vines with small berries.

J. F.'s Wheat

This round shape made by Jacob Furnival is similar to the **Wheat** shape, but has no ribs and is more detailed.

Jumbo

A round shape made by Henry Alcock with two elephant heads on the finials and chrysanthemums on the handles. Has been found in Tea Leaf as well as white ironstone.

Ladyfinger Ribs

Jean Wetherbee gives this term to the ribbed pieces popular in the 1870s and 1880s.

Lafayette Shape

Made by Joseph Clementson, border of swirls and leaves.

Lantern Hexagon

Early Classic Gothic shape, identified by Howard Noble in Jean Wetherbee's book.

Late Tulip

A shape made by Wedgwood & Co. which features a tulip sprouting out of either side of the bar finial.

Laurel "Shape"

Made by Wedgwood & Co. (Wedge Wood) in the 1860s.

Laurel Wreath "Shape" (Victory "Shape")

Registered by Elsmore & Forster in 1867, found also with the wreaths and bands decorated in Copper Lustre.

Jumbo mug by Henry Alcock & Co. 3" h., 3 1/4" dia.
Courtesy of Ernie & Bev Dieringer.

Adams Huron Shape Tea Leaf plate (9 1/2" dia.) shown with a covered vegetable in plain white ironstone (9" h., 11 1/4" handle to handle).
Courtesy of Dale Abrams.

Laurel Shape teapot by Wedgwood & Co. 10" h. *Courtesy of Dan Overmeyer.*

Laurel Wreath "Shape" three piece tea set by Elsmore & Forster. Teapot 9 1/2" h., sugar bowl 7 3/4" h., creamer 6" h. to lip. This shape was also called Victory "Shape" in 1867, but Dan Overmeyer and Gale Frederick speculate that for Southerners the Laurel Wreath shape name was more palatable. *Courtesy of Dan Overmeyer.*

Laurel Wreath "Shape" brush holder by Elsmore & Forster, missing the drainage/underplate, registered April 4, 1867. 6 1/2" h., 3" dia. *Courtesy of Dan Overmeyer.*

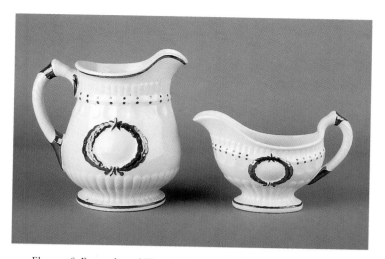

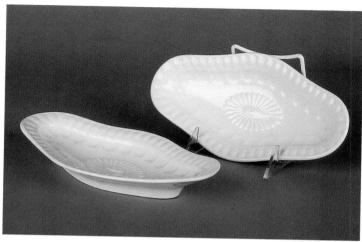

Elsmore & Forster Laurel Wreath "Shape" gravy boat (5" h.) and pitcher (8" h.) with highlights in Copper Lustre. *Courtesy of Dale Abrams.*

Laurel Wreath "Shape" relish dishes by Elsmore & Forster. 9" x 5". *Courtesy of Dan Overmeyer.*

Leaf and Crossed Ribbon

Made by Livesley & Powell, ca. 1850s-1860s. Has a design of leaves and bands across the piece, with foliage around the handle and spout.

Leaf Focus

Made by Taylor Bros., shape with a swirling band and a single leaf.

Lily of the Valley (James Edwards)

Registered by James Edwards in 1861. This round shape closely resembles Anthony Shaw's **Lily of the Valley**, but has flowers on only one side of the stems.

Lily of the Valley (Anthony Shaw)

Anthony Shaw registered made this shape in the 1860s. It is easily confused with James Edwards' **Lily of the Valley**; however, his shape has lilies on one side of the stem only, while Shaw's shape has lilies on both sides of the stems. Found in Copper Lustre Band and Tea Leaf.

Anthony Shaw Lily of the Valley coffeepot in Tea Leaf. 9 1/2" h. *Courtesy of Dale Abrams.*

Two sets of Anthony Shaw Lily of the Valley creamers (8" and 7 1/2" h.) and sugar bowls (6 1/2" and 5 1/2" h) in varying sizes. *Courtesy of Dale Abrams.*

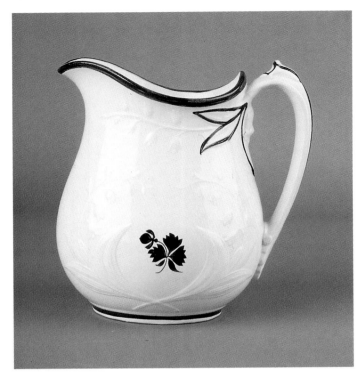

Anthony Shaw Lily of the
Valley pitcher. 8" h.
Courtesy of Dale Abrams.

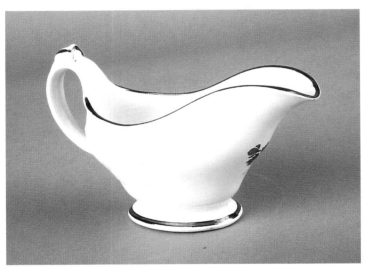

Anthony Shaw Lily of the Valley gravy boat. 5 1/4" h, 8 1/4" w.
Courtesy of Dale Abrams.

Anthony Shaw Lily of the Valley posset cups. 3 1/2" h.
Courtesy of Dale Abrams.

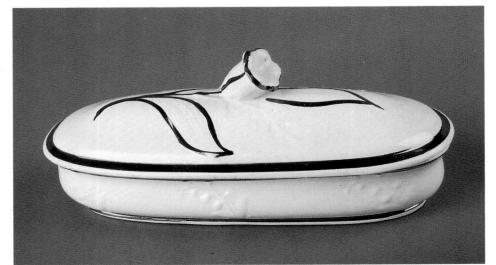

Lily of the Valley Tea Leaf brush box
by Anthony Shaw with Copper Lustre
but no Tea Leaf. 8 1/2" w., 3 1/2" h.
Courtesy of Dale Abrams.

80

Anthony Shaw Lily of the Valley mugs, 3 1/2" h. and 3 1/2" dia., 4" h. and 3 3/4" dia. *Courtesy of Dale Abrams.*

Anthony Shaw Lily of the Valley plate (9 1/2" dia.) with a cup plate (4" dia.) and a late, handled cup (3 3/4" dia., 3 3/8" h.). *Courtesy of Dale Abrams.*

Anthony Shaw Lily of the Valley soup tureen, covered butter dish, and soap dish with liner. Note that in Copper Lustre Lily of the Valley sometimes has a Tea Leaf motif and sometimes does not. The tureen is 10 1/2" h. and 10 1/2" handle to handle, the butter dish is 5" h., and the soap dish is 4 3/4" h. *Courtesy of Dale Abrams.*

Lily of the Valley with Thumbprints

A **Lily of the Valley** type shape with "thumbprints" (smooth, regular scalloped shapes approximating the shape a thumbprint might leave in the clay, see **New York Shape** for an example) around the base, made by Jacob Furnival.

Lily Shape (Burgess)

Shape decorated in calla lilies, made by Henry Burgess.

Lily Shape (Corn) *(see Bordered Hyacinth)*

Line Trim

Made by James Edwards and G. Wooliscraft, this is a shape with a simple border of lines.

Lion's Head

Made by Mellor Taylor & Co., ca. 1880s, this is a square shape with a lion's head in a medallion on the handles and finials. Found in Copper Lustre Tea Leaf.

Little Cable

Made by Thomas Furnival & Sons in the 1880s, this shape has a cable design with no ring. Found in Copper Lustre Tea Leaf only.

Little Pear

Looped shape made by John Alcock with a pear finial.

Long Hexagon

Six-sided **Classic Gothic** type shape made by J. Clementson, ca. 1845, and found in Mulberry.

Little Pear teapot by John Alcock. 8 1/2" h. *Courtesy of Dan Overmeyer.*

Furnival and Sons Little Cable coffeepot in Tea Leaf. 9" h. *Courtesy of Dale Abrams.*

Long Hexagon covered vegetable dish in Mulberry *Corea* pattern by J. Clementson. 8" h., 12 3/4" w. *Courtesy of Ellen R. Hill.*

Long Octagon

Made by Davenport, ca. 1845, found in Mulberry and Flow
Blue but not believed to have been made in plain white ironstone.

Long Octagon covered vegetable in Mulberry *Cologne*
by Alcock. 8" h., 12 3/4" w. *Courtesy of Ellen R. Hill.*

Rhone Scenery covered vegetable dish in Long Octagon. 7 1/2" h., 11 3/4"
handle to handle. *Courtesy of Ellen R. Hill.*

Long Octagon and Mayer"s Classic Gothic gravy boats in Mulberry
Rhone Scenery by T. J. & J. Mayer. Both are 5" h. *Courtesy of Ellen R. Hill.*

Long Octagon shape four-piece sauce tureen in Mulberry *Ning Po* by R. Hall. Notice the unusual ladle handle, which features a wonderfully embossed fierce-looking bird. 7 1/2" h., 8 1/2 handle to handle. *Courtesy of Ellen R. Hill.*

Loop and Dot

Looped shape by E. & C. Challinor, whose loops are separated at the bottom by circles.

Loop and Line

Made by Jacob Furnival, sparse loops and borders.

Maddock's Pear

Made by John Maddock, smooth round shape with leaves at the handles and a pear finial.

Below:
Maddock's Pear master waste jar by John Maddock.
16 1/2" h. *Courtesy of Ernie & Bev Dieringer.*

Maidenhair Fern

Shape manufactured by A. J. Wilkinson in the 1890s whose name comes from the wonderful fern leaves which drape on the handles and finials of pieces. As far as we know, this shape is only found in Copper Lustre Tea Leaf.

A. J. Wilkinson Maidenhair Fern mug. Note the detail on the handle. 3 1/2" h, 3 1/4" dia. *Courtesy of Dale Abrams.*

Maltese Shape (Mississippi Shape)

This shape named **Mississippi Shape** by E. Pearson and **Maltese Shape** by E. Corn appears to be the same as **Baltic Shape.**

Many Faceted

Sixteen-sided shape made by Davenport and Francis Morley & Co., ca. 1850s. Both makers have different finials on their pieces.

Many Panelled Gothic/Divided Gothic

Ten or more sided version of **Classic Gothic** made by John Alcock, Samuel Alcock, Clementson Bros., Elsmore & Forster, Anthony Shaw, and J. Heath ca. 1850s-1860s. This shape is found in Copper Lustre Band, the early stylized Tea Leaf, Teaberry, Mulberry, and Flow Blue. It may also be referred to as **Ten-Panelled Gothic** or **Classic Gothic Decagon.** See also **Twelve-Panelled Gothic.**

Many Panelled Gothic/Divided Gothic pitcher and wash bowl by John Alcock. Pitcher, 12" h., wash bowl, 14 1/2" dia. *Courtesy of Ernie & Bev Dieringer.*

Many Panelled Gothic soup tureen with underplate and ladle by John Alcock, ca. 1848-61. Underplate 14" by 12", soup tureen 12" h. x 11" w. *Courtesy of Ernie & Bev Dieringer.*

Mayer's Classic Gothic *(see Classic Gothic)*

Meadow Bouquet

Made by W. Baker & Co., floral design with ribbons and a cone finial.

Medallion Sprig

Made by Powell & Bishop, an outlined design of leaves and medallions.

Memnon Shape

Six-sided looped shape registered by John Meir & Son in 1857, with large embossed leaves around the handles and finials.

Mobile Shape

Many panels cover this shape by G. Bowers and J. Heath, and it is graced with a large flower finial.

Mocho "Shape"

Made by T. & R. Boote, a round shape with small decorations of flowers and leaves.

Montpelier

"Montpelier" is found on the bottom of some John Ridgway & Co. shapes—the term probably refers to a type of material used in the clay, and does not necessarily refer to the body style. However, different shapes identified by Jean Wetherbee using Montpelier in the name are **Montpelier Double Scallop** (this shape was also found in Mulberry, registered in 1848), **Montpelier Gothic**, **Montpelier Grape**, **Montpelier Graybeard**, and **Montpelier Hexagon**. The words "Porcelain a la Francaise" are also found on some of the pieces—despite the fact that Ridgway's White Ironstone was neither French nor porcelain!

Memnon shape teapot by J. Meir & Sons in 1857 (a pattern with different finials). 12" h. *Courtesy of Dan Overmeyer.*

Montpelier "Graybeard" pitcher with a bearded face under the lip. This piece is by John Ridgway & Co. and is listed as "Porcelaine a la Francaise". 8 1/4" h. at lip. *Courtesy of Dan Overmeyer.*

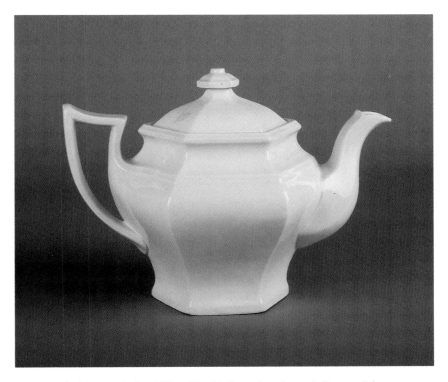

Teapot marked "Montpelier" and "Flow Blue, Mulberry, Porcelaine a la Francaise", by Ridgway, registered 1848. This piece may be referred to as Montpelier Hexagon. 8" h. *Courtesy of Dan Overmeyer.*

Morning Glory Shape *(see Halleck Shape)*

Morning Glory with Thumbprints

Unknown maker, round panelled shape with Morning Glory flowers and thumbprints around the bottom.

Moss Rose

Shape with roses and rope decorations, made by J. & G. Meakin.

Napier Shape

Neo-rococo decorated shape manufactured by Sampson Bridgwood & Son (Ltd.), ca. 1850s.

Napier shape teapots by Bridgewood & Son. 10" & 10 1/2" h. *Courtesy of Dan Overmeyer.*

Nautilus

Made by J. Clementson ca. 1840s-1850s, this wonderfully unique shape has a handle in the shape of a "nautilus shell" — some identify it as a nineteenth century stylized dolphin. This shape is found in Copper Lustre Band.

Four piece Nautilus sauce tureen in Copper Lustre on white ironstone, impressed J. Clementson. 7" h., 8 1/2" w. *Courtesy of Ellen R. Hill.*

New York Shape

This shape with panels, embossed leaves, thumbprints and a split pod finial was registered by J. Clementson in 1858 and can be found in Copper Lustre Band, Copper Lustre with Blue, Coral, and Teaberry.

New York Shape pieces shown in a display of Copper Lustre motifs: Copper Lustre with Flow Blue, Lustre Band, and Teaberry. *Courtesy of Dale Abrams.*

Niagara Fan

Registered by Anthony Shaw in 1856, this shape is thought to be one of the very first body styles be decorated with Tea Leaf. The name apparently stems from the similarity of Shaw's shape to Edward Walley's Niagara Shape. Found in Copper Lustre Band and Tea Leaf.

Anthony Shaw Niagara Fan coffeepot in Tea Leaf. 10" h. *Courtesy of Dale Abrams.*

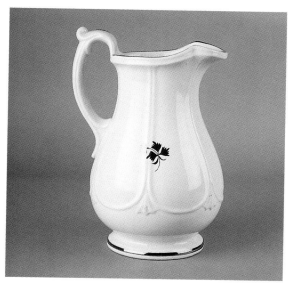

Niagara Fan Tea Leaf pitcher by Anthony Shaw. 11 1/4" h. to lip. *Courtesy of Dale Abrams.*

Niagara Fan teapot by Anthony Shaw, 1856. 10" h. *Courtesy of Ernie & Bev Dieringer.*

Anthony Shaw Niagara Fan sugar (7 1/2" h.) and creamer (5 1/2" h.) in Tea Leaf. *Courtesy of Dale Abrams.*

Anthony Shaw Niagara Fan plate (9 3/8" dia.), with two cup plates (4" & 4 3/4" dia.). *Courtesy of Dale Abrams.*

A rare Niagara Fan brush box by Anthony Shaw, 1856. 8" w., 3 1/4" h. *Courtesy of Dale Abrams.*

Niagara Shape

Registered by Edward Walley in 1856, found in Copper Lustre Band, Green Pre-Tea Leaf with Copper Lustre, Pinwheel, and Pomegranate.

Niagara shape in Pre-Tea Leaf, Lustre Band, and Pomegranate. *Courtesy of Dale Abrams.*

Nile Shape

Registered by Geo. L. Ashworth & Bros. in 1866, this shape is composed of a rope and lily pads with shell finials and handles.

Nine Leaf Fan (Ellen Hill)

Our Mulberry expert Ellen Hill named this **Classic Gothic**-style shape, made by Robert Hall & Co.

Six-sided Nine Leaf Fan creamer in Mulberry *Cologne*. 5 1/4". *Courtesy of Ellen R. Hill.*

Six-sided Nine Leaf Fan pitcher in Mulberry *Ning Po* by R. Hall. 7 1/2" h. *Courtesy of Ellen R. Hill.*

No Line Primary *(see Primary)*

Nosegay

A pattern of ribbons and flowers are found on this shape by E. & C. Challinor.

90

Nut with Bud

Round shape made by John Meir & Son, with leaves around the handles and spout, and a nut finial.

Olympic Shape

Registered in 1864 by Elsmore & Forster, this shape had a Greco-Roman style border pattern and a pagoda finial.

One Large and Two Little Ribs

This shape is composed of alternating ribs in different sizes, made ca. 1870s by Elsmore & Forster, J. & G. Meakin, and T. & R. Boote.

Oriental Shape

Made by W. E. Corn, this shape has a rope around the top and a floral pattern around the base and handle.

Pacific Shape

This many sided shape with an acorn finial was made by Elsmore & Forster in 1871.

Panelled Berry with Leaves

Made by J. & G. Meakin, this is a many sided shape with scalloped edges and foliage on the handle and spout.

Panelled Columbia

Lively and Powell, J. Clementson, E. & C. Challinor, G. Wooliscroft, J. Meir & Son, Elsmore & Forster, W. Adams, and Pennman Brown & Co. are some of the makers of this shape which is a variation of **Columbia Shape** but with panels and shields.

One Large and Two Little Ribs compote by Elsmore and Forster, 1853-1871. Note that there are two sizes larger than this one. 5 3/4" x 4" h. Courtesy of Ernie & Bev Dieringer.

Oriental Shape teapot by W. E. Corn, 1864-91. 10 1/2" h. Courtesy of Ernie & Bev Dieringer.

Panelled Columbia toothbrush holder with undertray by Joseph Goodwin. 5" h., 3" dia., 4 1/4" dia undertray. *Courtesy of Dan Overmeyer.*

Panelled Grape

Makers included Jacob Furnival, Edward Pearson, Chas. Meigh & Son, Joseph Clementson, and J. Goodwin, ca. 1860s. Some finials are ring shaped while others are in the shape of a grape cluster. This shape can be found in Copper Lustre Band, Botanical, Cinquefoil, Pinwheel, and Teaberry as well as Mulberry.

Panelled Grape pieces in Lustre Band, Botanical, and Teaberry. *Courtesy of Dale Abrams.*

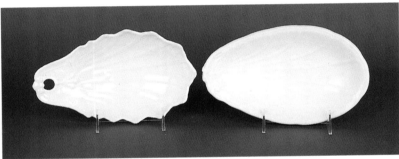

A relish dish with leaf and bud design (shape name and maker unknown, 9" l.), is shown to the left of a Panelled Grape relish dish by J. Goodwin. 9 1/4" l. *Courtesy of Ernie & Bev Dieringer.*

Panelled Leaves

Panelled shape with leaves at the handle, made by J. & G. Meakin.

Panelled Lily

Made by Jacob Furnival and J. W. Pankhurst, a panelled shape similar to Sydenham with a flower finial.

Panelled Pod

Many sided shape made by J. & G. Meakin, with a pod finial.

Paris Shape

Patented in 1857 by John Alcock and later made by Henry Alcock. Its gourd finial makes this shape unique.

Paris Shape gravy boat by Henry Alcock, 1857. 9 3/4" x 5 1/2" h. *Courtesy of Ernie & Bev Dieringer.*

Peach

Shape with crabstock handles and a peach-shaped finial, made by George Wooliscroft.

Pear

Made by Anthony Shaw in the late 1860s, with a pedestaled and a regular base. Can be found in Copper Lustre Band and Tea Leaf.

Anthony Shaw Pear coffeepot and sugar bowl. Teapot is 8 3/4" h. *Courtesy of Dale Abrams.*

Shown here are two different treatments of the same Pear sugar bowl, Copper Lustre enhanced on a pedestal on the left (7 1/2" h), and Copper Lustre Tea Leaf on the right (6 1/2" h). *Courtesy of Dale Abrams.*

Pearl Sydenham

Variation on the popular Sydenham Shape made by J. & G. Meakin. Also note that W. Pearson's **No. 5 Shape** uses exactly the same body but was given a different name by the maker.

Pearson's No. 5 Shape *(see Pearl Sydenham)*

Pearson's No. 6 Shape

This shape by E. Pearson is very similar to James Edwards' **Ball and Stick**.

Peerless "Shape" (Feather)

Registered by John Edwards in 1887, a square style with long panels separated by feathers (according to *Handbook of Tea Leaf Body Styles*, this may have been in honor of the Edward VII, the Prince of Wales, who visited the pottery). This shape is not known to have been made in plain white ironstone.

Persia Shape

Made by E. Corn, a panelled shape with a nut finial.

Pharoh Cameo

Made by J. & G. Meakin, this round shape had a Pharoh's head on the handles and the finial.

Pie Crust *(see Blanket Stitch)*

Pearl Sydenham teapot by Meakin, marked "Paris White Ironstone" on the base. 9 1/2" h. *Courtesy of Dan Overmeyer.*

Pinch-Neck Gothic

Classic Gothic-style shape with a pinched-in neck, made by James Edwards ca. 1847. This shape can be found in Mulberry and Flow Blue. It is also called **Full Panel Pinch-Neck** by some collectors.

Pinch-Neck Gothic teapot by James Edwards. 8 1/4" h. *Courtesy of Dan Overmeyer.*

Pinch-Neck Gothic teapot in Mulberry *Bochara* pattern by J. Edwards. 8 1/4" h. *Courtesy of Ellen R. Hill.*

Pinch-Neck Gothic teapot in Flow Blue *Coburg* pattern by James Edwards. 8 1/4" h. *Courtesy of Gale Frederick and Dan Overmeyer.*

Plain Berlin

Plain round shape made ca. 1860s by Liddle, Elliott & Son.

Plain Round: Bulbous

This simple but elegant shape has no embossing. It was made by many potters, including Alfred Meakin & Co., J. & G. Meakin, W. & E. Corn, Henry Burgess, Burgess & Goddard, William Baker, Baker & Chetwynd, E. & C. Challinor, A. J. Wilkinson, and Thomas Elsmore & Son. The *Handbook of Tea Leaf Body Styles* points out the distinction between this "bulbous" set and the children's sets, which include a bulbous and a tapered shape, made by Mellor Taylor (ca. 1880s-1890s). This shape can be found in Copper Lustre Tea Leaf and Gold Lustre Cloverleaf, Morning Glory, and Tea Leaf.

Plain Round teapot with a pewter handle and lid. It is marked patented June 27, 1876, with a "Hiffe" name beneath the date. This unusual piece has not been documented before now. 9 1/2" h. *Courtesy of Dan Overmeyer.*

Wedgwood and Co. Plain Round veritcal toothbrush holder in Tea Leaf. 5" h. *Courtesy of Dale Abrams.*

Plain Round syllabub bowl in Tea Leaf by H. Burgess. 5 3/4" h., 8 3/4" dia. *Courtesy of Dale Abrams.*

Plain Round Tea Leaf footed compote, unmarked. 5" h., 8 1/4" dia. *Courtesy of Dale Abrams.*

Plain Round Alfred Meakin mush bowl in Tea Leaf. *Courtesy of Dale Abrams.*

Anthony Shaw Plain Round veritcal toothbrush holder in Tea Leaf. 5" h. *Courtesy of Dale Abrams.*

A. J. Wilkinson Plain Round veritcal toothbrush holder in Tea Leaf. 5 3/4" h. *Courtesy of Dale Abrams.*

Plain Scallop *(see Crystal)*

Plain Uplift

Term which describes the basic round shape with uplift handles manufactured by many potters ca. 1870-1900.

Plum Decagon

Made by J. & G. Meakin, this ten-sided shape has crabstock handles (on the tureens) and a large plum finial.

Pomegranate

This shape has a similar border to **Trent Shape**, and has dividing loops. It was made by Jacob Furnival & Co.

Polonaise

Made by Edge-Malkin & Co. in the 1880s, Polonaise is found in Tea Leaf; the ironstone in this shape is usually a creamy, buttery color.

Poppy Shape (Scotia Shape)

Shape similar to **Prairie Shape** made by both Frederick Jones & Co. and J. & C. Wileman. The difference is that the Poppy Shape has concave ribs instead of **Prairie Shape's** wider, rounder melon ribs.

Portland Shape

Made by Elsmore & Forster and Elsmore & Son, ca. 1850s, this shape can be found in Morning Glory, Reverse Teaberry, and Green & Copper Lustre.

Potomac Shape (Blackberry)

Made by W. Baker & Co., registered in 1862. Round shape covered in blackberry leaves and berries, divided at the neck.

Prairie Flowers

First designed by Livesley & Powell ca. 1860, then made by Powell and Bishop in the 1870s. **Wheat in the Meadow**, a later pattern by Powell & Bishop, uses similar embossing. Can be found in Copper Lustre Band and Pomegranate.

Rarely found in white, this is an unusual Edge Malkin Polonaise cup and saucer in Tea Leaf. Edge-Malkin pieces are normally an creamy, yellowish color. 2 3/4 h", 4" dia. *Courtesy of Dale Abrams.*

Elsmore & Forster Portland Shape coffeepots in Reverse Teaberry and Morning Glory. 10 1/4" h. *Courtesy of Dale Abrams.*

Prairie Shape

Registered by J. Clementson and also made by Clementson Bros. A very popular shape, perhaps because it appealed to the American "new frontier" market. Found in Lustre Band, Cinquefoil, Coral, and Teaberry.

Prairie Shape pieces shown in Teaberry, Coral, and Lustre Band. *Courtesy of Dale Abrams.*

President Shape

John Edwards registered this panelled shape with **Sydenham**-like shields in 1855 and 1856.

Above:
President shape by John Edwards, 1855, soup tureen with underplate and matching ladle. The soup tureen is 13" h. x 11", and the underplate is 13 1/4" x 14 1/2". *Courtesy of Ernie & Bev Dieringer.*

Right:
President Shape butter dish by J. Edwards. 7 3/4" dia., 5" h. *Courtesy of Ernie & Bev Dieringer.*

99

Primary (Single Line/Double Line/No Line/Belted)

This very popular style, ca. 1845, was made in six- and eight-sides, and with a double line, single line, no line, and belted. Makers of **Single Line Primary** include T. J. & J. Mayer, T. Walker, E. Challinor, and F. & R. Pratt. This shape is one of the most common in Flow Blue, and can also be found in Mulberry (though rare).

Makers of **Double Line Primary** include Davenport, Alcock, J. Wedge Wood, Wood & Brownfield, Mellor & Venables, Heath, Fell, Challinor, Furnival, Mayer, and Maddox. It can be found in Mulberry and Flow Blue.

No Line Primary was made by Podmore Walker, J. Goodwin, Hughes, J. Meir & Sons, and can be found in Mulberry and Flow Blue.

Belted Primary was made by Alcock, found in Mulberry.

Single Line Primary teapot in *Arabesque*, Flow Blue, made ca. 1851 by T. J. & J. Mayer. 8 1/2" h. *Courtesy of Gale Frederick and Dan Overmeyer.*

Three-piece Flow Blue *Oregon* pattern teaset by Mayer in No Line Primary. Teapot 9 3/4" h. *Courtesy of Gale Frederick and Dan Overmeyer.*

Single Line Primary teapot in Mulberry *Scinde* pattern by Thomas Walker. 10 1/2" h. *Courtesy of Ellen R. Hill.*

"Belted" Primary in Mulberry *Vincennes* by Alcock. 8 1/2" h. *Courtesy of Ellen R. Hill.*

Single Line Primary teapot with acorn finial in Mulberry *Lady Peel* by Francis Morley & Co. This teapot has also been seen in *Casmir* (a Flow Blue pattern). 8 1/2" h. *Courtesy of Ellen R. Hill.*

Double Line Primary in Flow Blue *Chapoo* by John Wedge Wood, ca. 1850. 11 1/2" h. teapot. *Courtesy of Gale Frederick and Dan Overmeyer.*

Beauties of China pattern in Flow Blue, Double Line Primary teapot, marked, by Mellor Venable and Co. Teapot 11 1/2" h. *Courtesy of Gale Frederick and Dan Overmeyer.*

Prize Bloom

Registered in 1853 by T. J. & J. Mayer, also made by James Edwards. This shape, popular with collectors, is distinctive because of its wonderful three-dimensional flower finial. It was probably named "Prize" because of the award it received at the Crystal Palace Exhibition in London in 1851. Found in Mulberry.

Prize Bloom six-sided tea set in Mulberry *Flower Vase* six-sided pattern by T. J. & J. Mayer in blue, rose, and green polychrome. 9 1/2" h. teapot, 7 1/2" h. sugar, 6" h. creamer. *Courtesy of Ellen R. Hill.*

Prize Bloom six-sided, covered vegetable dish in Mulberry *Rhone Scenery* by T. J. & J. Mayer. 7 1/2" h., 10 1/2" handle to handle. *Courtesy of Ellen R. Hill.*

Flow Blue *Oregon* pattern vegetable dish in Prize Bloom, ca. 1853 by T. J. & J. Mayer. 7 1/2" h. *Courtesy of Gale Frederick*

Prize Bloom teapot by T. J. & J. Mayer. The back stamp lists Dale Hall pottery and Prize Medal 1851. 9 1/4" h. *Courtesy of Dan Overmeyer.*

Prize Bloom lidded pitcher by James Edwards. 6 3/4" h. *Courtesy of Dan Overmeyer.*

Prize Bloom tureen with undertray (shown with a Sydenham ladle). 8" h. x 8" w., 9" w. handle to handle on undertray. *Courtesy of Dan Overmeyer.*

Prize Nodding Bud (Narrow-Waist Gothic)

Jean Wetherbee calls this shape Prize Nodding Bud, but Ellen Hill calls it Narrow-Waist Gothic. Registered by T. J. & J. Mayer in 1851, found in Mulberry.

Narrow-Waist Gothic teapot shown in Mulberry *Rhone Scenery* by T. J. & J. Mayer. Note the very nice handle, made in two pieces with an extra flair at the top. 9 1/4" h. *Courtesy of Ellen R. Hill.*

Prize Puritan

Registered by T. J. & J. Mayer in 1851, this shape is unique because of the low band around the bottom of the body and the crown finial. This shape also derives its name from a prize medal it won in 1851.

Prize Puritan in Mulberry *Flower Vase* by T. J. & J. Mayer in blue, rose, and green polychrome. 9 1/2" h. teapot, 8" h. sugar, 6" h. creamer. *Courtesy of Ellen R. Hill.*

Prize Puritan pitcher and wash bowl and creamer by T. J. & J. Mayer, ca. 1851. Pitcher, 10 1/2" h., wash bowl, 13 1/2" dia., creamer 5" h. *Courtesy of Ernie & Bev Dieringer.*

Prunus Blossoms

Made ca. 1880s by Henry Alcock & Co., divided border of flowers and Greco-Roman lines.

Pumpkin (Hexagon, Octagon, and Decagon)

Made by T. J. & J. Mayer ca. 1853, found in Mulberry and Flow Blue.

Pumpkin Primary shape teapot in Mulberry *Pelew* (a pattern which was not supposed to have been made in Pumpkin) by Challinor. 8 1/2" h. *Courtesy of Ellen R. Hill.*

Furnival's Ten-Panelled Pumkin Primary teapot in Flow Blue *Shanghae.* 8 1/2" teapot. *Courtesy of Gale Frederick and Dan Overmeyere.*

104

Ten-Panelled Pumpkin Primary teapot and creamer in Mulberry *Rhone Scenery* by T. J. & J. Mayer. 8" h., 6" h. *Courtesy of Ellen R. Hill.*

Quartered Rose

Made by Jacob Furnival, ca. 1860, this shape is named for its rosebud finial. Found in Copper Lustre Band, Pinwheel, Teaberry, and Copper Lustre with Blue and Red Band.

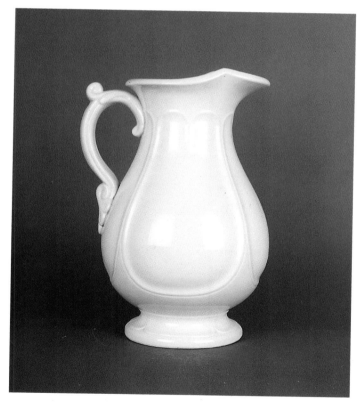

Quartered Rose pitcher by Jacob Furnival. 10 3/4" h. *Courtesy of Ernie & Bev Dieringer.*

Quartered Rose covered pitcher by J. Furnival & Co., with an unusual mark on the bottom. 10" h. *Courtesy of Dan Overmeyer.*

Quartered Rose pieces in Pinwheel and two pieces of Blue and Red Pinstripe with Copper Lustre. *Courtesy of Dale Abrams.*

Reeded Grape

Registered on 1855 by Pankhurst and Dimmock, this divided shape has many vertical ribs with a grape design around the neck.

Regalia

Square/oblong shape made by S. F. & J. ca. 1890s, with corner embossing that resembles a crown. Found in Copper Lustre Tea Leaf only.

Ribbed Berry

Made by both John Alcock and Henry Alcock.

Ribbed Berry mug by Henry Alcock. 3" h., 3 1/4 dia. *Courtesy of Ernie & Bev Dieringer.*

Ribbed Bud

Made by J. W. Pankhurst, similar to **Full Ribbed**, with buds on the finials.

Ribbed Chain

Made by J. W. Pankhurst, with small ribs, a chain, and a branch finial.

Ribbed Fern

Ribs with a fern pattern make up this A. J. Wilkinson shape.

Ribbed Grape

Shape by W. & E. Corn, ribbon with vertical grape vines and leaves.

Ribboned Oak

Ribbed shape with embossed raspberries by J. & G. Meakin.

Richelieu "Shape"

Made by James Wileman, ca. 1870s, this round shape has striped finials. It has been found in Copper Lustre Morning Glory, but has not been found in plain white ironstone.

Ring O'Hearts

Made by Livesley & Powell and Jacob Furnival, registered 1853. This bulbous shape is divided, with heart shapes above the ridges which give it this name. Found in Copper Lustre Band, Pinwheel, Teaberry, and Mulberry.

Rococo

Made by many potters, ca. 1840s+, this shape, found normally in porcelain, can also be found in Gold Lustre Cloverleaf and Morning Glory. This is an embossed, elaborate rococo style shape which sometimes is found on a pedestal.

Rolling Star

Made by James Edwards, this shape has a gentle rolling line around the border, giving the appearance of a large, wide star.

Rondeau

Made by Davenport, ca. 1870s-1880s, and found in Copper Lustre Band and Tea Leaf. There are no known pieces in plain white.

Davenport Rondeau coffeepots, the one on the left is in Copper Lustre Tea Leaf, on the right is Copper Lustre Band. 9 1/2" h. *Courtesy of Dale Abrams.*

Davenport Rondeau waste bowl and three piece butter dish. Dish 5 3/4" h., bowl 3 3/4" h. and 5 1/2" dia. *Courtesy of Dale Abrams.*

Davenport Rondeau creamer and sugar bowl. Creamer 6" h., sugar bowl 6 1/2" h. *Courtesy of Dale Abrams.*

107

Roped Wheat (The Lorne)

Registered in 1878 by Thomas Furnival and Sons, the border is an elaborate series of wheat, leaves, ropes, and bows.

Rope with Melon Ribs

Panelled piece with a nicely embossed rope circling the neck, made by J. & G. Meakin.

Round Teardrop (Ellen Hill)

This shape, identified by Ellen Hill, was made ca. 1859 by John Thomson & Sons, and as far as we know is only found in Mulberry.

Royal "Shape" (Lion's Head/Sheepshead)

Made by John Edwards ca. 1870s, named Royal by the maker but nicknamed "Lion's Head" or "Sheepshead" due to the shape found on the handles and finials of some pieces. Made in Copper Lustre Tea Leaf, though rare.

Royal Shape (Henry Alcock & Co.)

This shape is a bit of a mystery—it is marked "Royal" in the manufacturer's mark, but is somewhat different from the Edwards' Lion's Head Royal "Shape".

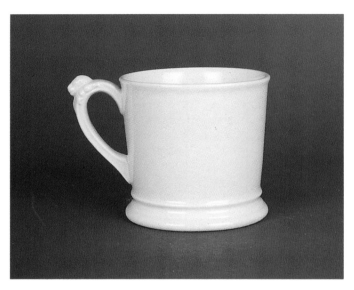

Royal "Shape" mug by John Edwards. 3 1/2" h., 3 1/2" dia. *Courtesy of Ernie & Bev Dieringer.*

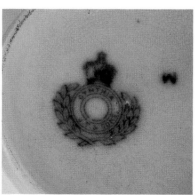

Round Teardrop teapot in *Cynthia* by J. Thomson & Son. 9". *Courtesy of Ellen R. Hill.*

Safety Pin

Made by J. & G. Meakin with panels/loops in the shape of safety pins.

Scalloped Decagon/Cambridge Shape

Made by both John Wedge Wood (marked J. Wedgwood) and Davenport in the 1850s. Because we find so many shapes made by both Wedgwood and Davenport only, Jean Wetherbee speculates that the two manufacturers may have "shared" shapes at some point (p. 106).

Scalloped Decagon/Cambridge Shape mug by Davenport, ca. 1853. 3 1/4" h., 3 1/2" dia. *Courtesy of Ernie & Bev Dieringer.*

Scalloped Decagon by J. Wedge Wood, 1853. 8 3/4" h. *Courtesy of Dan Overmeyer.*

Left:
Scallop Decagon soup tureen by Davenport, ca. 1856. Soup tureen is 10" h., 10" w., underplate is 16" x 11". *Courtesy of Ernie & Bev Dieringer.*

Scotia Shape *(see Poppy Shape)*

Scroll

This shape, made by Alfred Meakin ca. 1870s, is believed to be this prolific maker's earliest shape decorated in Tea Leaf. There are scroll decorations at the handles and finials. Not known to have been made in plain white ironstone.

Scroll Border

Made by Sampson Bridgwood & Son, this shape has a border of scrolls and swirls.

Scrolled Bubble

Made by J. W. Pankhurst, this eight-panelled shape has embossed scrolls and leafy decorations.

Two Scrolled Bubble teapots by J. W. Pankhurst. Note that the smaller shape, with a different finial, is not as nicely potted.11 1/4" h. and 10" h. *Courtesy of Dan Overmeyer.*

Seine "Shape"

This shape by John Edwards has a bar finial with a pointed, elegant design.

Senate "Shape"

Registered by T. & R. Boote, a plain round shape with elaborate handles. A very similar, if not the same, shape is listed in *Handbook of Tea Leaf Body Styles* as made by Henry Burgess, Alfred Meakin, Mellor Taylor, and A. J. Wilkinson ca. 1870s in Copper Lustre Tea Leaf.

Sevres Shape

Made by John Edwards, a round shape with embossed foliage around the spout and the floral handles, found with cone and nut finials.

Sharon Arch

Made by John Wedge Wood (J. Wedgwood) and Davenport, this shape has a scrolled/leafy border and handles.

Shield

Registered by Anthony Shaw, this shape is actually a semi-porcelain with a cream color, found in Copper Lustre Tea Leaf only.

Simple Pear

This bulbous shape was made by Alfred Meakin, ca. 1880s, and has large C-shaped handles. As far as we known, this shape is found only in Copper Lustre Tea Leaf.

Simple Square

This term refers to plain pieces in a square shape. Simple but elegant shapes like this were made beginning ca. 1870s by many English and American manufacturers. Simple Square pieces were often decorated in Tea Leaf (Gold Lustre as well as Copper Lustre). The *Handbook of Tea Leaf Body Styles* describes three types of **Simple Square**: **Pagoda** (named for the arch finial), **Puffy** (named for the large, bulging body), and **Wedgwood's Plain** (made by Enoch Wedgwood, with a recessed base, tapered dishes, and a low waist on pitchers).

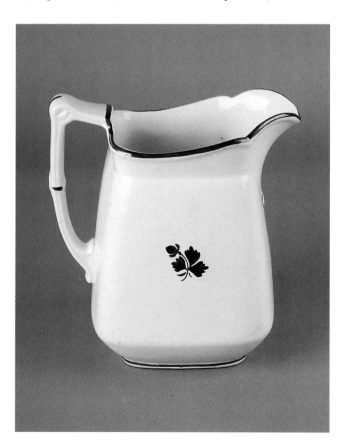

(Enoch) Wedgwood Simple Square milk pitcher. *Courtesy of Dale Abrams.*

110

Simple Square sugar bowl in Tea Leaf by Wedgwood & Co. (Enoch Wedgwood). 6 1/4" h. *Courtesy of Dale Abrams.*

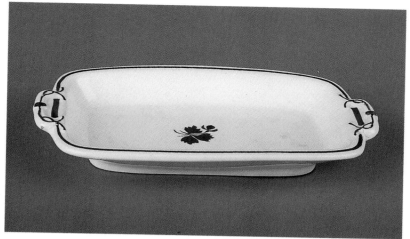

(Enoch) Wedgwood & Co. Simple Square relish dish. 8 1/4" w. *Courtesy of Dale Abrams.*

Simplicity

Made ca. 1880s by Anthony Shaw and Powell & Bishop, a round style with uplifted handles found in Copper Lustre Tea Leaf by Shaw and Copper Lustre Rose by Powell & Bishop.

Six-Panelled Trumpet (and Elaborate Six-Panelled Trumpet)

Made by J. W. Pankhurst, six framed sides with a leaning trumpet flower finial.

Split Pod

Panelled shape with a handle ending in a leaf, by James Edwards.

Square Open Flower

Registered in 1848 by James Edwards, a very similar shape to **Square Rosebud**.

Square Open Flower teapot by James Edwards, marked Dec. 16, 1848. 8 1/2" h. *Courtesy of Dan Overmeyer.*

Square Ridged

Nancy Upchurch has divided this shape name into five groups. The first is **Beaded Handle**, registered by Henry Burgess and was made in Copper Lustre Tea Leaf. The handles have a beaded underside.

Hearts, made ca. 1880s by Mellor Taylor & Co., was also made in Copper Lustre Tea Leaf and its distinguishing features include a heart-shaped motif on the finials and handles.

Iona was made by Powell, Bishop & Stonier registered 1886, and has ridges at the bottom of pieces, and was found decorated with a Gold Lustre Tea Leaf motif.

Square Pear, made ca. 1880s-1890s by W. & E. Corn, has a scalloped rim and was decorated in Copper Lustre Tea Leaf and Gold Lustre Cloverleaf and Tea Leaf.

Wedgwood's Ribbed was made by Wedgwood & Co. ca. 1880s, and in a reproduction by Red Cliff in the 1960s. This is the most common of the **Square Ridged** shapes, and also has a ribbed bottom and bracket feet. It is found in Copper and Gold Lustre Tea Leaf.

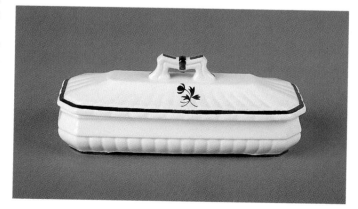

Red Cliff Square Ridged (Wedgwood's Ribbed) brush box. 9 1/2" x 3". *Courtesy of Dale Abrams.*

Henry Burgess veritcal toothbrush holder in a Square
Ridged (Beaded Handle) body style. 6" h. *Courtesy of
Dale Abrams.*

Red Cliff Ironstone China Advertising Plaque (this 20th century
American manufacturer had a full line of Tea Leaf). Tea Leaf in
Square Ridged (Wedgwood's Ribbed) sauce tureen by Red Cliff,
1950s-1960s. Some Red Cliff designs are near exact copies of
19th c. pieces—this is a copy of a (Enoch) Wedgwood piece.
Plaque 8 3/8" dia., sauce tureen 4 3/4" h., 8" handle to handle,
undertray 7 3/8" w. *Courtesy of Dale Abrams.*

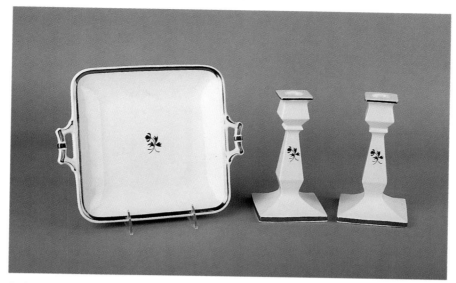

Red Cliff low pedestalled compote and candlesticks—this is very unusual, as we do not find Tea Leaf candlesticks in the 1800s! The cake plate is a reproduction of Square Ridged (Wedgwood's Ribbed) shape. 10 1/2" w. handle to handle, 2 1/4" h. Candlesticks 7 1/2" h. *Courtesy of Dale Abrams.*

Square Rosebud

Square shape registered in 1848 by James Edwards with a rosebud finial.

Square Tumbling Petals

Square shape also registered in 1848 by James Edwards, with an acorn finial and flower with falling petals on the handle.

St. Louis Shape

Made by John Edwards, this shape features both a melon-shaped finial and a thick flower finial.

Stafford Shape

Registered by Samuel Alcock & Co. in 1854, this large panelled shape is very similar to John Alcock's **Trent Shape**.

Star Flower

Made by J. W. Pankhurst, this body is covered in a small floral pattern and has a gourd or fruit finial.

Sunburst

This shape, found only (thus far) in Copper Lustre Tea Leaf, was made by A. J. Wilkinson ca. 1880s-1890s. Its sunburst handles and finials give it this name.

Summer Garden

Made by George Jones, this shape was decorated in large and small groups of flowers and leaves.

St. Louis Shape toothbrush holder by John Edwards. 7 3/4" x 3 1/4". *Courtesy of Ernie & Bev Dieringer.*

Swags & Scroll

Potter unknown, ca. 1850s, found in the Pre-Tea Leaf motif and Copper Lustre and Blue, not known to have been made in plain white.

Swag and Scroll Blue and Copper creamer, 7" h. *Courtesy of Dale Abrams.*

Sydenham Shape

One of the most popular shapes in white ironstone, registered by T. & R. Boote in 1853.

Sydenham Shape tea set by T. & R. Boote, 1853. Teapot, 10 1/4" h.; sugar bowl, 7 1/2" h.; creamer, 6" h.; waste bowl, 4" h., 5 1/4" dia. *Courtesy of Ernie & Bev Dieringer.*

Sydenham Shape tea set, featuring a rare large teapot. Largest 10 1/2" h.; smaller 9 3/4" h.; 7 1/2" h. sugar; 5 1/4" h. to lip of creamer. *Courtesy of Dan Overmeyer.*

Boote's Sydenham Shape table pitchers in three sizes. 8" h., 9 1/4" h., 10 1/4" h.
Courtesy of Ernie & Bev Dieringer.

Sydenham Shape pitchers. The largest is 10 1/2" h.,
creamer 5" h. to lip. *Courtesy of Dan Overmeyer.*

Three mugs in Sydenham Shape by T. & R. Boote, ca. 1853. A child's
mug, 2 7/8" h. x 3 1/4", shaving mug, 3 3/8" h. x 3 7/8", and a cider mug,
3 5/8" h. x 4 1/8". *Courtesy of Ernie & Bev Dieringer.*

Sydenham Shape creamers in three sizes. 5" h., 5 1/2" h., 6 1/2" h.
Courtesy of Ernie & Bev Dieringer.

Eleven Sydenham Shape posset or syllabub cups. 4" h., 2 7/8" dia.
Courtesy of Dan Overmeyer.

Sydenham Shape
chowder tureen by T.
& R. Boote. 8 3/4" h.
*Courtesy of Dan
Overmeyer.*

116

Sydenham soup tureen by T. & R. Boote (was made in at least three sizes). Soup tureen 14 1/2" h., 10" w.; underplate 16" w. at handles. *Courtesy of Dan Overmeyer.*

Pictured here is possibly the smallest covered vegetable dish that has ever been seen, in Sydenham Shape. Note that the difference between this and a chowder tureen is that the chowder does not sit upon a pedestal and the covered vegetable does not have handles. 8" h., 8" dia. *Courtesy of Dan Overmeyer.*

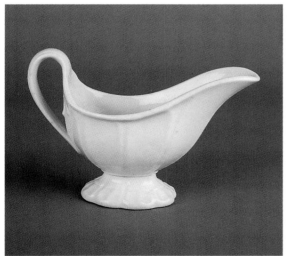

Sydenham Shape gravy boat. 5" h. at lip, 8 1/2" wide. *Courtesy of Dan Overmeyer.*

Sydenham Shape oval covered vegetable dish by T. & R. Boote. 9 1/4" h., 11" w. *Courtesy of Dan Overmeyer.*

Sydenham Shape sauce tureen with underplate and ladle. Sauce tureen is 7" h., 6" w.; underplate 8 1/2" x 7". *Courtesy of Ernie & Bev Dieringer.*

Sydenham Shape toilet set by T. & R. Boote. Chamber pot with lid 8" dia., 7 3/4" h.; shaving mug 3 3/4" dia., 3 3/8" h.; vertical brush holder 5" h.; soap dish with insert, 3 1/2" h., 5" w.; brush box 3 1/4" h., 8" w.; pitcher 11 1/2" to lip; wash bowl 13 1/2" dia., 5" h. A larger pitcher was available for the wash bowl. *Courtesy of Dan Overmeyer.*

Sydenham Shape pitchers in two sizes (a third 12" pitcher is known to exist, but is not pictured here). 11 1/2" h., 13" h. *Courtesy of Ernie & Bev Dieringer.*

Sydenham Shape pitcher and wash bowl by T. & R. Boote, 1853. The octagon pitcher is 11 1/2" h., bowl is 13" dia. *Courtesy of Ernie & Bev Dieringer.*

Sydenham Shape covered butter dish including liner. 5" h, 7 1/2" dia.
Courtesy of Ernie & Bev Dieringer.

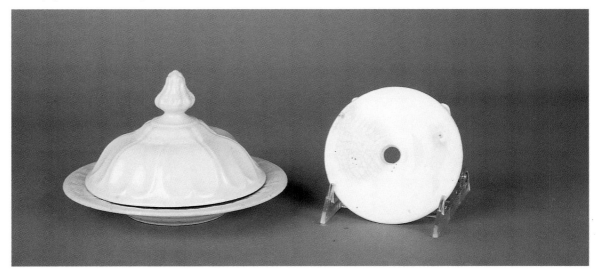

Sydenham Shape butter dish by T. & R. Boote, 1853. 5" h., 7 1/2" dia.
Courtesy of Dan Overmeyer.

Sydenham Shape oval fruit compote by T. & R. Boote. 7 1/2" h., 11 1/4" w. *Courtesy of Dan Overmeyer.*

Sydenham Shape round fruit compote by T. & R. Boote. 7 1/2" h., 10 3/8" dia. *Courtesy of Dan Overmeyer.*

Anthony Shaw Sydenham soup plate, a very early example. The first year Tea Leaf is believed to have been made is generally thought to be 1856, but the back mark on this piece predates this. This green motif may be a Tea Leaf motif experiment. 10 1/2" dia. *Courtesy of Dale Abrams.*

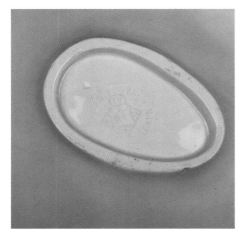

Sydenham Shape (leaf shape) relish by T. & R. Boote, 1853. 9" x 6 1/2". *Courtesy of Ernie & Bev Dieringer.*

Ten-Panelled Gothic *(see Classic Gothic Decagon)*

Tiny Oak and Acorn

Made by J. W. Pankhurst, this round shape is covered in oak leaves.

Tracery

Made by the Johnson Bros. (Hanley) Ltd., this shape with scroll decorations was made after 1883.

Trailing Ivy

This shape by John Maddock & Sons featured forked handles ending in ivy.

Trent Shape

Made in 1854 by Samuel Alcock. Note that there is a similarity to the **Stafford** shape, made by John Alcock. This shape was also decorated in Flow Blue.

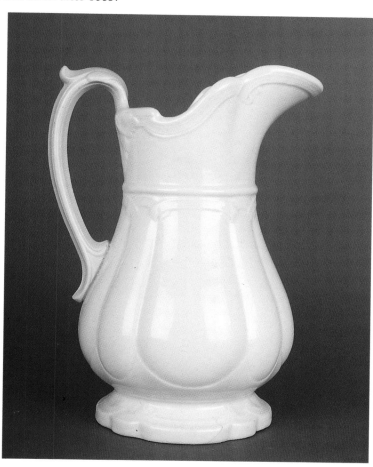

Trent Shape pitcher by John Alcock. 11 1/4" h. *Courtesy of Ernie & Bev Dieringer.*

Trent Shape teapot by John Alcock. The shape is also found in the Flow Blue *Scinde* pattern. 9 1/4" h. *Courtesy of Dan Overmeyer.*

Triple Border

Shape by James Edwards with three lines for a border and grape cluster handles.

True Scallop

Scalloped shape made by various potters in the mid-nineteenth century, including James Edwards, E. & C. Challinor, and John Alcock.

Trumpet Vine

Registered by Liddle, Elliot & Son in 1865. This shape has large embossed groupings of foliage and flowers.

Tulip "Shape" (Little Scroll)

Registered in 1862 by Elsmore & Forster, this shape is found in Blue and Copper Lustre, Copper Lustre Band, Tea Leaf, Tobacco Leaf, and Flow Blue.

Tuscan Shape

Made by John Edwards in 1853, this shape is covered in lines and floral decorations.

Twelve-Panelled Gothic

Similar to **Many Panelled Gothic**, this shape was registered in 1853 by Venables Mann & Co. Has a ring handle and rose finial.

Twelve-Panelled Ridged

This shape identified by Ellen Hill, was made by Thomas Furnival Son(s) and T. Fell, and can be found in Mulberry and Flow Blue.

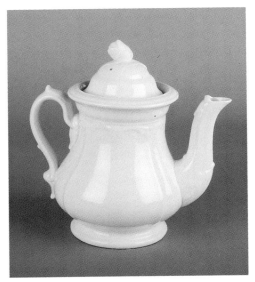

Three examples of Tulip "Shape" by Elsmore & Forster, shown in Lustre Band and two examples of Blue and Copper Lustre. *Courtesy of Dale Abrams.*

Tulip "Shape" teapot by Elsmore & Forster. 9 1/4" h. *Courtesy of Dan Overmeyer.*

Tulip "Shape" Blue and Copper Lustre tea set. Teapot 8 1/2" h. *Courtesy of Dale Abrams.*

Tulip "Shape" gravy boat and covered vegetable dish. Gravy boat is 8 1/2" w., 5" h.; the covered vegetable is 7" x 10" x 7". *Courtesy of Louise and Charles Loehr, Louise's Old Things, Kutztown, Pennsylvania.*

Tulip "Shape" tea set in Flow Blue and Copper Lustre. Teapot 8 3/4" h. *Courtesy of Louise and Charles Loehr, Louise's Old Things, Kutztown, Pennsylvania.*

Twelve-Panelled Ridged creamer in Mulberry *Wreath* by T. Furnival. 5 1/2" h. *Courtesy of Ellen R. Hill.*

Twelve-Panelled Ridged pitcher in polychrome. *Phantasia/Wreath* pattern, by one of the Furnivals. 11" h. *Courtesy of Ellen R. Hill.*

123

Twin Leaves Hexagon

Registered by James Edwards in 1851, very similar to **Flowered Hexagon**, which was registered on the same day by the same maker.

Twisted Ribbon

Shape with a border design of a twisted ribbon which reveals a flower, made by James Edwards ca. 1860s.

Union Shape

Made by T. & R. Boote, bulbous-like shape divided just below the waist.

Union Shape pitcher and wash bowl by T. & R. Boote. The pitcher is 12" h., and the wash bowl is 14" dia. *Courtesy of Ernie & Bev Dieringer.*

Twin Leaves Hexagon teapot by James Edwards, marked August 29, 1851. 8 1/4" h. *Courtesy of Dan Overmeyer.*

Vertical-Panelled Gothic

Variation of **Classic Gothic** made by Charles Meigh & Son and Mellor Venables & Co., and probably a few other potters as well. This is a popular shape in Mulberry and Flow Blue.

Vertical-Panelled Gothic teapot in Mulberry *Athens* pattern by Charles Meigh. 8 1/2" h. *Courtesy of Ellen R. Hill.*

Vertical-Panelled Gothic teapot in Mulberry *Beauties in China* by Mellor Venables. (This teapot is often called a coffee pot.)9 3/4" h. *Courtesy of Ellen R. Hill.*

Vertical-Panelled Gothic wash bowl and pitcher in *Brunswick* by Mellor Venables, decorated in two shades of orange polychrome. This is an unusual piece, as *Brunswick* is normally found in rose, blue, and green colors. This is the only pieces like this that Ellen Hill has ever seen. 16" w., 14" h. *Courtesy of Ellen R. Hill.*

Vertical-Panelled Gothic pitcher in Mulberry *Whampoa* by Mellor Venables. 9" h. *Courtesy of Ellen R. Hill.*

Vertical-Panelled Gothic master slop jar, also in the rare orange polychrome *Brunswick*. 17" h. *Courtesy of Ellen R. Hill.*

125

Vertical-Panelled Hexagon

This shape name refers to six-sided versions of **Vertical-Panelled Gothic**, made by Davenport.

Victor Shape

Registered by F. Jones & Co. in 1868, decorated in corn wreaths and thumbprints. A similar shape to **Laurel Wreath**.

Victorian Beauty

Made by E. & C. Challinor, ca. 1880s, a round shape with scalloped edges; so far it has only been found in Copper Lustre Tea Leaf.

Victory "Shape" (Dolphin)

Registered by John Edwards, the dolphin-like handles and finials on this shape are what give it its name. It is a popular shape in both Copper Lustre Tea Leaf and plain white ironstone.

Victory "Shape" mug by John Edwards. 3 1/4" h., 3 1/4" dia. *Courtesy of Ernie & Bev Dieringer.*

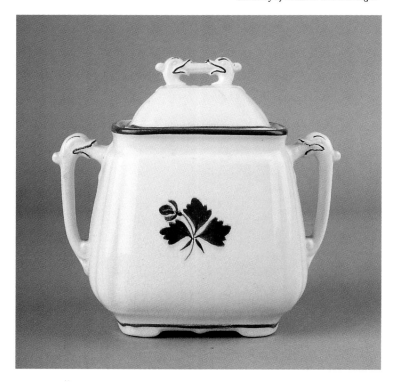

John Edwards Victory "Shape" (Dolphin) sugar bowl. 7" h. *Courtesy of Dale Abrams.*

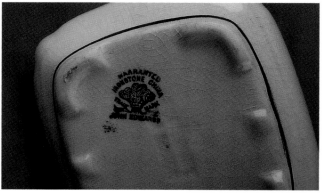

John Edwards Victory "Shape" (Dolphin) soup tureen. *Courtesy of Dale Abrams.*

Victory "Shape" *(see Laurel Wreath "Shape")*

Vintage Beauty

This rare shape, with decorations of grapes and leaves, was made by Anthony Shaw ca. 1860s. It can be found in Copper Lustre Tea Leaf.

Vintage Shape

Shape made by William Adams and E. & C. Challinor, ca. 1860s. Round design of medallions and leaves, with a chain border. Can be found in Copper Lustre Tea Leaf.

Walled Octagon

Made by Jacob Furnival & Co. ca. 1850s, an octagonal shape with concave panels and a large pod finial. It is found (though rare) in Copper Lustre Band.

Washington Shape

Registered by John Meir & Son in 1863 and Powell & Bishop in 1869. Found in Copper Lustre Band, Rose, and Pomegranate. Some of the motifs are also entirely Copper Lustre tinted green or have green parts.

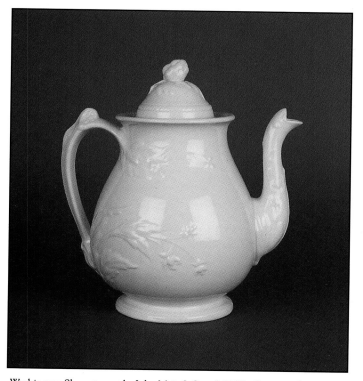

Washington Shape teapot by John Meir & Son. 9 3/4" h. *Courtesy of Ernie & Bev Dieringer.*

127

Powell & Bishop Washington Shape teapot in the Rose motif. 9 1/2" h. *Courtesy of Dale Abrams.*

Washington Shape mug by John Meir & Son. 3 3/4" dia., 3 3/4" h. *Courtesy of Ernie & Bev Dieringer.*

Western Shape

Registered by Hope & Carter in 1862, this shape has a border pattern of twisted lines and flowers.

Wheat

This shape, similar to **Ceres**, was made by Mellor, Taylor & Co., David Methven and Sons, Hollinshead & Kirkham, A. J. Wilkinson, W. & E. Corn, Henry Meakin, and W. Baker & Co. This is very different from the **Wheat** made by Jacob Furnival.

Wheat

Made by Jacob Furnival, ca. 1860s. A round shape with no panels and a wheat border, which can be found in Copper Lustre Cinquefoil.

Wheat and Clover

A shape with wheat, clovers, ribbons, and foliage made by Tomkinson Bros. & Co., Turner & Tomkinson, Taylor Bros., and Ford, Challinor & Co.

Wheat and Daisy

Made by Bishop & Stonier, William Adams & Sons, and Johnson Bros. (Hanley) Ltd. This shape had a border of alternating wheat and daisy designs.

Wheat and Hops

Panelled shape with thumbprints and embossed wheat and hops design, made by J. & G. Meakin (Ltd.), Jacob Furnival & Co., William Taylor, Robert Cochran & Co., Alfred Meakin (Ltd.), E. Pearson (he called his "**Ceres Shape**"), W. E. Oulsnam & Son, Clementson Bros, and St. Johns Chinaware Co. (a Canadian maker).

Wheat and Rose

Panelled shape with wheat and rose designs made by Alfred Meakin (Ltd.) in the late nineteenth and early twentieth centuries.

Wheat Harvest

By John Alcock, pre-1861, this shape has a wheat handle and designs, and an apple finial.

Wheat Harvest Shape by John Alcock. 3 1/2" h., 3 3/4" dia. *Courtesy of Ernie & Bev Dieringer.*

Wheat in the Meadow

Registered in 1869 by Powell & Bishop, this round shape has two wheat designs on pieces, and can be found in Copper Lustre Band and Rose.

White Oak and Acorn

Round panelled shape by Holland & Green, covered in oak, vine, and acorn designs.

Wild Rose Twig

Round/bulbous shape made by Charles Meigh & Son, 1860+. Large flower finial and handles.

Winding Vine

Registered by T. & R. Boote in 1867, this is a shape with a border of vine.

Winterberry

A shape made with leaves and a pod finial.

Woodland

Made by W. & E. Corn, ca. 1890s, a round/bulbous shape with floral and rope designs. It is found in Copper Lustre Tea Leaf.

Wrapped Sydenham (Double Sydenham)

A very popular shape made by Livesly & Powell, Anthony Shaw, Edward Walley, Holland & Green, W. & E. Corn, John Maddock & Sons (Ltd.), and Thomas Goodfellow, ca. 1850s. It is found in Copper Lustre Band, Lustre Scallops, Tea Leaf, and Green & Copper Pre-Tea Leaf, and Mulberry.

Wrapped Sydenham teapot in Mulberry *Marble* pattern by Anthony Shaw. 9 1/2" h. *Courtesy of Ellen R. Hill.*

Small Tea Leaf covered dish in Wrapped Sydenham by Anthony Shaw. *Courtesy of Dale Abrams.*

Wrapped Sydenham pieces in Lustre Band, Pre-Tea Leaf, and Scallops. *Courtesy of Dale Abrams.*

Generally, most collectors are interested more in British made ironstone than that which was made in the United States. There was a prejudice against American wares during the nineteenth century, and perhaps it is because of this that American pieces are normally not given shape names. However, there were a few very notable American makers of white ironstone, and some very popular makers who decorated their pieces with Copper Lustre. These include J. & E. Mayer, East End Pottery, J. & E. Mayer, and American Crockery Co. More modern makers are Red Hall (which copied British shapes, and so can be found in the shapes listings) and Kitchen Craft, by Homer Laughlin. The following is a sampling of pieces made by these makers. You may also find American examples in the Miscellaneous chapter.

J. & E. Mayer creamer in Tea Leaf. 5 1/4" h. to lip. *Courtesy of Dale Abrams.*

J. & E. Mayer coffeepot in Tea Leaf. 8 3/4" h. *Courtesy of Dale Abrams.*

Kitchen Craft covered vegetable dish in the Tea Leaf motif. 4" h. *Courtesy of Dale Abrams.*

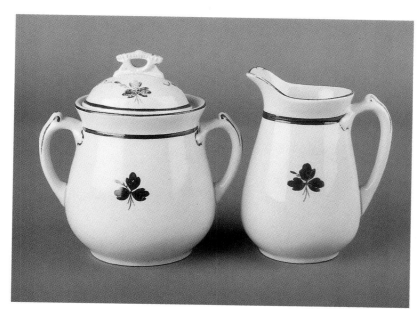

East End Pottery creamer (6 1/2" h) and sugar bowl (7 1/4") in Tea Leaf. *Courtesy of Dale Abrams.*

Gold Lustre Tea Leaf American Crockery Co. cup and saucer 2 3/4" h. and 3 1/2" dia. *Courtesy of Dale Abrams.*

Tea Leaf Kitchen Craft container by Homer Laughlin. 7 1/4" h. *Courtesy of Dale Abrams.*

Pie plate (9 1/2" dia.) and salt and pepper shakers (3" h.) by Kitchen Craft in Tea Leaf. *Courtesy of Dale Abrams.*

Compotes

Floral "Open Flower" compote, unmarked.
8" dia., 4" h. *Courtesy of Dan Overmeyer.*

Unidentified fruit
compote by Davenport.
7" h. x 10". *Courtesy of
Ernie & Bev Dieringer.*

Leaf compote by American potter William Brunt, ca.1865-78. 4 1/4" h. x 9" w. *Courtesy of Ernie & Bev Dieringer.*

Many panelled small fruit compote by James Edwards. 3" h.
Courtesy of Dan Overmeyer.

Unknown shape and maker, opened handled, pedestalled compote.
8" h., 12 1/2" handle to handle. *Courtesy of Dan Overmeyer.*

"Grapes and Leaves" shape
compote by J. & E. Mayer of
Beaver Falls, Pennsylvania.
9 1/2" dia, 5 3/4" h. *Courtesy
of Dan Overmeyer.*

Mulberry and Staffordshire blue transfers fruit bowl in *Warwick* by J. & M. P. Bell. This is an extremely rare piece. 5 1/2" h., 11" handle to handle. *Courtesy of Ellen R. Hill.*

Lily Pad tri-footed stand by Pankhurst & Co., ca. 1856.
9 1/2" dia. x 3" h. *Courtesy of Ernie & Bev Dieringer.*

Scalloped fruit bowl by T. & R.
Boote. 8" dia. x 4" h. *Courtesy of Ernie & Bev Dieringer.*

Fluted apple bowl by Cockson & Seddon, Cobridge.
10" dia, 5 1/4" h. *Courtesy of Dan Overmeyer.*

Pinwheel decorated berry bowl. 5 1/4" dia.
Courtesy of Gale Frederick.

Alfred Meakin Fluted footed apple bowl in Tea Leaf. 4" h., 9 1/2"
dia. *Courtesy of Dale Abrams.*

Unknown shape relish dish by Barrow & Co., 1853-1856. 9" x 6 1/2". *Courtesy of Dan Overmeyer.*

Shell shaped master server and individual servers (relish dishes) by T. & R. Boote, ca. 1851. 10 3/4", 8" long to handles. *Courtesy of Dan Overmeyer.*

Fish shape relish dish by J.M. (JF?) & Co. 9 1/2" l. *Courtesy of Dan Overmeyer.*

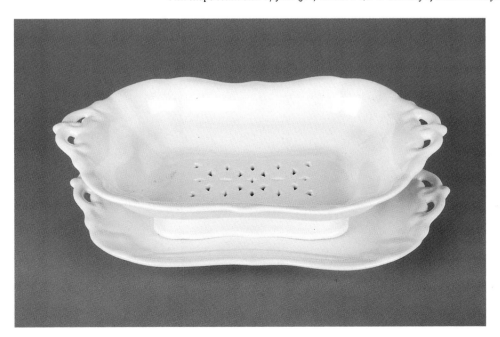

Unknown shape chestnut server with undertray by Petrus Regout and Co. 12" w. handle to handle. *Courtesy of Dan Overmeyer.*

Above:
"Cupped hands" shape relish dish by Knowles, Taylor & Knowles. Shown here with two different marks which have been found on the same piece. 7 1/2" long. *Courtesy of Dan Overmeyer.*

Hands in Flow Blue sponge. 7" x 5 1/4". *Courtesy of Ernie & Bev Dieringer.*

Relish dish made by the American East End Pottery, from Liverpool, Ohio. 9 1/2" w. *Courtesy of Dale Abrams.*

Grapes and grape leaves design relish dish by
Davenport, marked 1860 in anchor. 9 1/4" w.
Courtesy of Dan Overmeyer.

"Pierced Scroll" reticulated fruit bowl and its flowing blue *Scinde* pattern
decorated counterpart. 13 1/4" w., 3 1/2" h. *Courtesy of Dan Overmeyer.*

Nicknamed "Pierced Scroll" reticulated fruit dish and undertray, attributed to J. & G. Alcock but
unmarked. 13 1/2" handle to handle, 3 3/4" h. bowl, 11" w. undertray. *Courtesy of Dan Overmeyer.*

Unknown shape reticulated undertray. 10 3/4" x 8 3/4".
Courtesy of Dan Overmeyer.

This reticulated fruit bowl with a separate underplate was made by T. & R. Boote. Note that the handles are missing. Jean Wetherbee calls this "Arcaded Square". Bowl 11" x 9" x 4" h, underplate also 11" x 9". *Courtesy of Dan Overmeyer.*

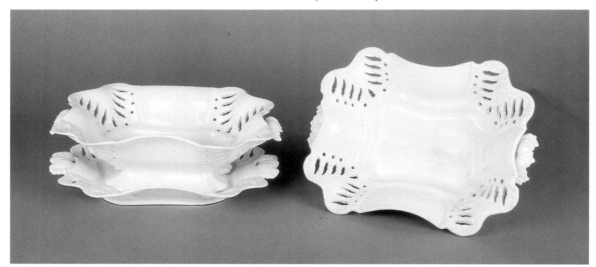

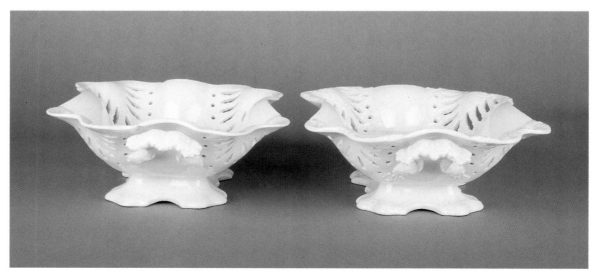

Two reticulated fruit bowls with undertrays (unknown shape), one is decorated with a lot of embossed detail while the other is left quite plain. Appears in the *Rhone* pattern by Thomas Furnival in Flow Blue and also in *Indian Jar* by Jacob and Thomas Furnival in Flow Blue. 12" w. undertray, 12" w. bowls, 3 3/4" h. handle to handle. *Courtesy of Dan Overmeyer.*

Jean Wetherbee called this shape "Heart and Diamonds", a reticulated undertray by E. Challinor, seen in plain white ironstone. 13 1/2" x 10". *Courtesy of Dan Overmeyer.*

Undertrays in plain white and Flow Blue *Indian Jar. Courtesy of Dan Overmeyer.*

Unknown shape reticulated compotes which have been seen marked by Shaw and by Edwards. 10" dia, 9 1/2" h. 10 1/4" dia., 5 1/4" h. *Courtesy of Dan Overmeyer.*

Three footed reticulated fruit or chestnut bowl in Mulberry *Athens* pattern by Charles Meigh. Note the feet, which have four well-defined toes! This is a very rare piece in Mulberry. 4 1/2" h., 9" dia. *Courtesy of Ellen R. Hill.*

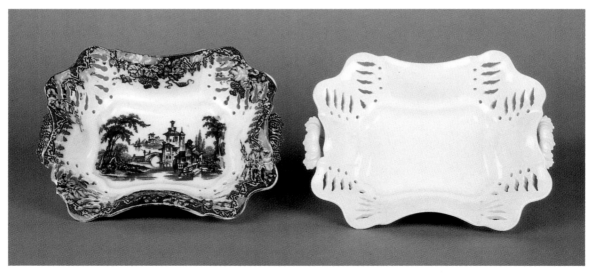

White reticulated fruit bowl shown with its *Rhone* pattern Flow Blue decorated counterpart. *Courtesy of Dan Overmeyer.*

Cake stand in Mulberry *Udina* pattern by J. Clementson, unusual because of its four feet (as opposed to a singlr low pedastal). 2 1/2" h., 12" dia. *Courtesy of Ellen R. Hill, with special thanks to the generosity of Brad and Jane Nelson.*

Edge Malkin Tea Leaf cake plate in the usual buttery yellow color. 10" w. *Courtesy of Dale Abrams.*

Fluted cake stands in three sizes, the largest and smallest are by Jacob Furnival, and the middle one is possibly by W. & S. Largest is 12" dia., 5" h; middle 9 3/4" dia. x 4 1/2" h; smallest 6 3/4" dia, 3 1/4" h. *Courtesy of Dan Overmeyer.*

J. & E. Mayer cake plate in Tea Leaf. 11 1/4" w. handle to handle. *Courtesy of Dale Abrams.*

Unidentified shape cake stand with a glass lid by Davenport, ca. 1869, with a glass lid. This unidentified shape has a shell decoration on the stand. 9" dia. x 10" h. *Courtesy of Ernie & Bev Dieringer.*

146

J. & E. Mayer Tea Leaf egg cup. 4" h.
Courtesy of Dale Abrams.

Three unmarked egg cups in Copper Lustre Tea Leaf, the smaller one is a
particularly unusual size (2 1/2" h). 3 1/2 and 3 1/4" h. *Courtesy of Dale
Abrams.*

Alfred Meakin Boston egg cups in the Tea Leaf motif. 1 3/4" h, 4" dia.
Courtesy of Dale Abrams.

Egg cups. 2 1/2" h., 2" dia. *Courtesy of Dan Overmeyer.*

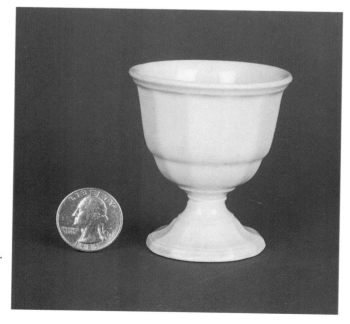

Early Gothic egg cup,
unknown maker. 2 1/2" h.
x 2 1/4" dia. *Courtesy of
Ernie & Bev Dieringer.*

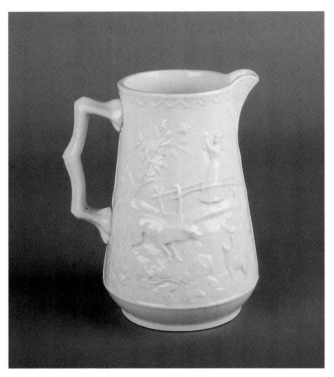

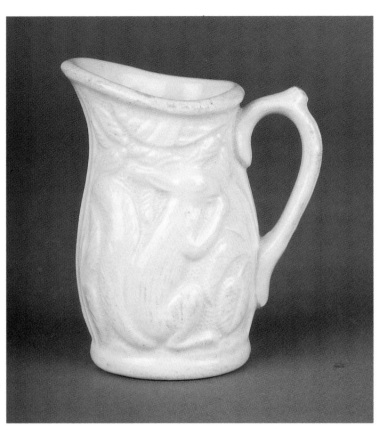

Heavily embossed pattern with a dog, sheep, and a little girl, unmarked. 8" h. at the lip. *Courtesy of Dan Overmeyer.*

A 4" high small jug in an embossed squirrel pattern. *Courtesy of Dan Overmeyer.*

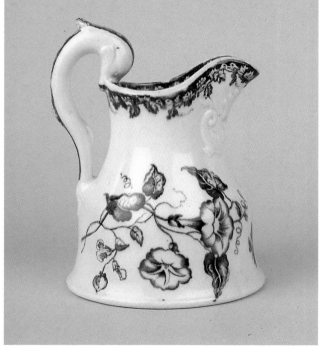

A very unusual shape, a dolphin handled pitcher in Mulberry *Vine Border (Morning Glory)* by J. & M. P. Bell. Note also the trident under the lip. 6 3/4" h. *Courtesy of Ellen R. Hill.*

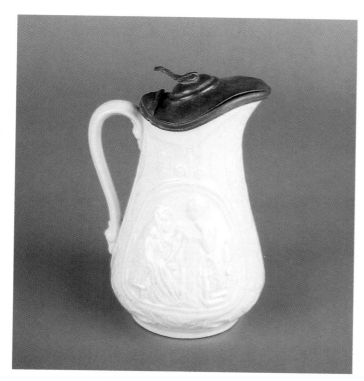

High relief pitcher with pewter lid, unmarked. 7 1/4" h. to lip. *Courtesy of Dan Overmeyer.*

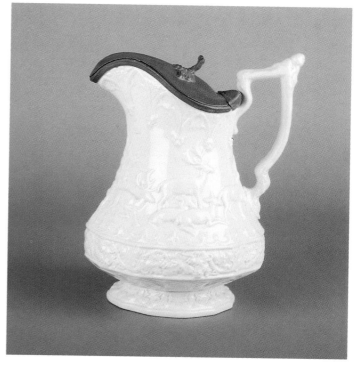

Heavily embossed hunting scene with deer and dogs, capped with a pewter lid. 9" h. at lip. *Courtesy of Dan Overmeyer.*

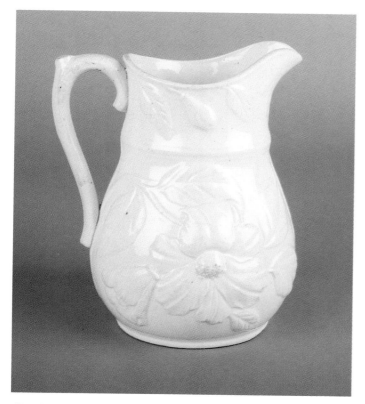

Heavily embossed floral pattern with open flowers and buds. 7" h. at lip. *Courtesy of Dan Overmeyer.*

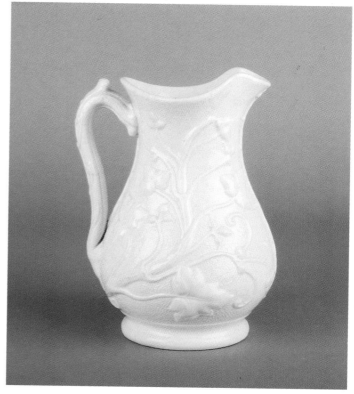

Pitcher with ivy vines. 9" h. at lip. *Courtesy of Dan Overmeyer.*

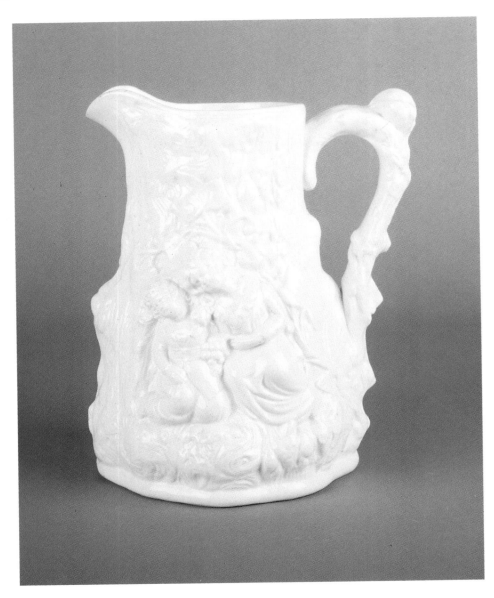

Jean Wetherbee named this embossed pitcher "Babes in the Woods" by Cork & Edge. 9" h. to the lip. *Courtesy of Dan Overmeyer.*

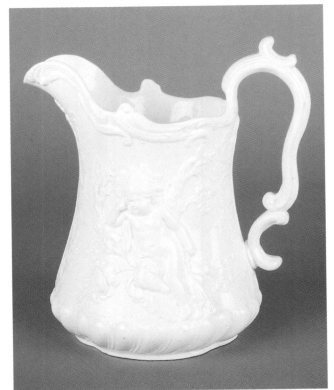

Embossed pitcher by Cork & Edge. 8" h. to the lip. *Courtesy of Dan Overmeyer.*

150

Basket and floral motif child's teapot with a pewter lid, shown with an adult-size teapot in an embossed pattern with swags, plants, and leaves, capped with a pewter lid. Child's teapot, 3 1/2" h., adult-sized teapot, 9" h. *Courtesy of Dan Overmeyer.*

This "Trunk with Ivy" mug by Cork & Edge gets its name from its unusual tree shape. 4" h. x 3 3/4" dia. *Courtesy of Ernie & Bev Dieringer.*

Unknown shape platter with a deer's head, oak leaf and acorn, and entwined twig motif by J. M. & Co. 14 1/2" w. *Courtesy of Dan Overmeyer.*

Jean Wetherbee named this highly ornate and unmarked jug "Favorite Grostesque". Notice the details of the faces and on the handle. 8" h. to the base of the lip. *Courtesy of Dan Overmeyer.*

Shown here is a pair of polychrome candlesticks in *"Flower Sprig"* (Ellen Hill's pattern name) made by Woode & Brownfield. 7 1/2" h. *Courtesy of Ellen R. Hill.*

Lavender transfer smoker's set, also called the "Bachelor's Companion", maker unknown. This six piece set consisted of a tobacco jar, tobacco weight, spittoon/ashtray, candlestick, goblet, and a pipe tamper. This example is missing the pipe tamper, which would have fit onto the top of the set. 26 1/4" h. *Courtesy of Ellen R. Hill.*

Chamber stick with snuffer holder, the candle snuffer is missing. 3 1/4" h., 6" dia. *Courtesy of Dan Overmeyer.*

Candlestick, impressed "Registered 11th July 1846". 9 1/4" h. *Courtesy of Dan Overmeyer.*

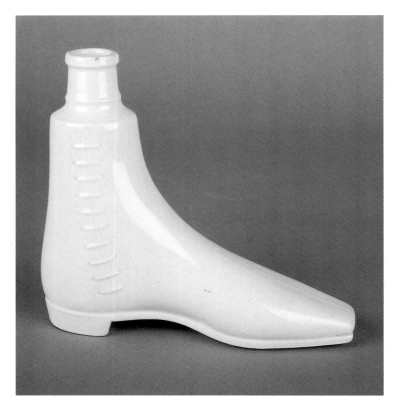

Boot flask, 7 1/2" long, 6 1/2" h. *Courtesy of Dan Overmeyer.*

Flask in the shape of a smiling man, spout in top of cap. 7" h. *Courtesy of Dan Overmeyer.*

Tea Leaf spittoon by Anthony Shaw. Note the faces. 3 1/2" h., 8 1/4" dia. *Courtesy of Dale Abrams.*

Flask in the form of a dog. 6 1/4" h. *Courtesy of Dan Overmeyer.*

Tea Leaf cuspidor by Anthony Shaw.
This is the only example like this
known in Tea Leaf. 7" h., 7 1/2" w.
Courtesy of Dale Abrams.

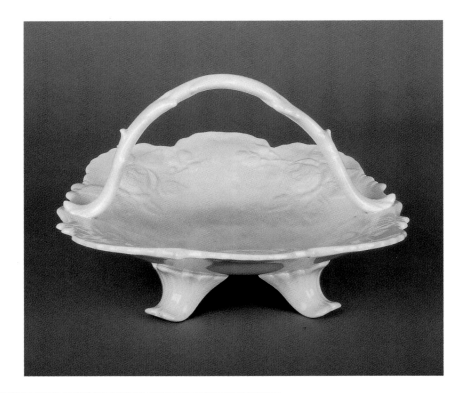

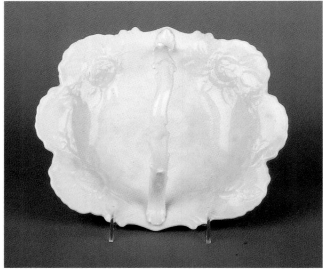

Jean Wetherbee named this basket "Open Roses", made by James Edwards. 5 1/2" h., 10" w. *Courtesy of Dan Overmeyer.*

Ladies' cuspidor in Flow Blue *Coburg* pattern by James Edwards, 3 1/2" h., 3 3/4" dia. opening. *Courtesy of Dan Overmeyer.*

Nautilus shell spoon warmer with feather edge brush stroke.
7 1/2" w., 4 3/4" h. *Courtesy of Margot Frederick.*

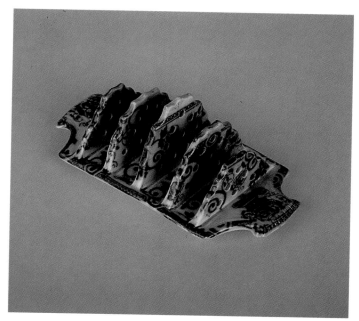

Toast rack in Flow Blue *Basket* pattern. *Courtesy of Dan Overmeyer.*

Toast rack by J. Clementson, 9 1/4" w.
Courtesy of Dan Overmeyer.

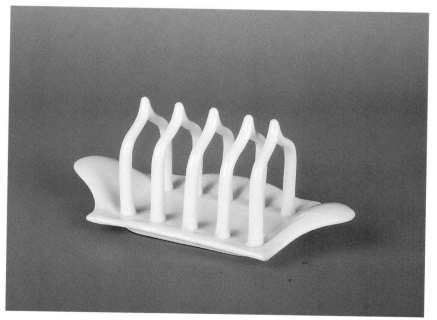

Hot water plate in Flow Blue *Berry* pattern, by William Ridgway, ca.
1840. 10 1/4" dia., 2 3/8" h. *Courtesy of Dorothy and Arnold Kowalsky.*

Master salt, 1 3/4" h., 2" d. *Courtesy of Dan Overmeyer.*

Mulberry *Marble* flask with a multi-colored transfer made by
F. & R. Pratt (artist signed). 7" h. *Courtesy of Ellen R. Hill.*

Very unusual double-spouted server in Mulberry *Rose* by T. Walker
believed to be a fish sauce, part of a fish set. 5 1/4" h. *Courtesy of
Ellen R. Hill.*

Shell spoon warmer, maker unknown. 7 1/2" w, 4 1/2" h.
Courtesy of Dan Overmeyer.

Two mustard pots: Eagle (Diamond Thumbprint) on the left (4" h.),
unidentified shape on right *Courtesy of Dan Overmeyer.*

Mustard pot with attached undertray. 4 1/4" h., undertray 5" w.
Courtesy of Dan Overmeyer.

"Fern" shape cheese bell, unmarked. 9" h., 11" dia.
Courtesy of Dan Overmeyer.

Hen on Nest, unmarked. 9" w., 8 1/2" h. *Courtesy of Dan Overmeyer.*

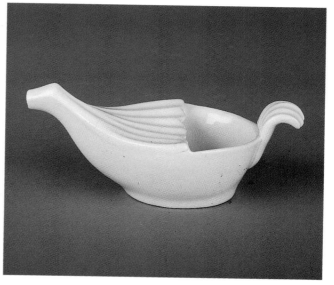

Invalid feeder. 5 1/2" l. *Courtesy of Dan Overmeyer.*

Hot water plate in Mulberry *Clematis* by Davenport. Hot water would have been poured into the opening on the side, where a stopper in a matching pattern was fitted to a cork (some stoppers were also attached to the piece by a chain). These were most likely used to keep plates warm on a sideboard (although some collectors believe they were used to keep the actual food warm). 10" dia. *Courtesy of Ellen R. Hill.*

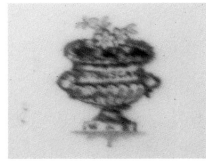

Mulberry *Etruscan* hot water plate by Wood & Brownfield. 10" dia. *Courtesy of Ellen R. Hill.*

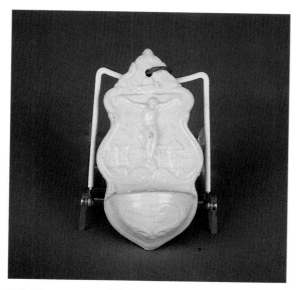

Holy Water container. 6" h. *Courtesy of Dan Overmeyer.*

Unknown shape storage jar, unmarked. 7 3/4" h.
Courtesy of Dan Overmeyer.

A rare foot bath in Mulberry *Geddo* by Adams (one of the most common
patterns found in Mulberry). 9 1/2 h., 22" w. *Courtesy of Ellen R. Hill.*

Framed Leaf foot bath
by Pankhurst. 16 3/4"
x 12 1/2" x 9" h.
*Courtesy of Ernie &
Bev Dieringer.*

By Shape

Ceres Shape child's tea set by Elsmore & Forster with plates, creamer, sugar bowl, teapot, waste bowl, and handled cups and saucers. Teapot, 5 1/4" h. *Courtesy of Dan Overmeyer.*

No Line Primary child's set (also seen in *Scinde* in Flow Blue), attributed to J. & G. Alcock. Teapot, 4" h.; sugar, 3 1/2" h.; creamer, 2 3/4" h. to lip; cups, 2 3/8" h. x 2" dia.; saucers, 4 1/4" dia. *Courtesy of Margot Frederick.*

Classic Gothic Decagon child's partial tea set by W. B. & Co. which is also
marked P W for Pearl White. 5" h. teapot. *Courtesy of Dan Overmeyer.*

Columbia Shape partial child's tea set by Elsmore &
Forster, ca. 1855. Teapot, 5" h. *Courtesy of Dan Overmeyer.*

Double Line Primary child's teapot, sugar bowl, and
creamer. Teapot, 5 1/2" h. *Courtesy of Dan Overmeyer.*

Double Line Primary teapots, child's-sized and full-sized. The full-sized teapot is marked G. Phillips, Longport, Pearl Ironstone. 9" h., child's teapot, 5 1/2" h. *Courtesy of Dan Overmeyer.*

Fig child's teapot and sugar bowl. Teapot, 5 3/4" h. *Courtesy of Dan Overmeyer.*

Child's teapots in three shapes: Panelled Lily, the ever-popular unidentified, and Grape Octagon. Left to right: 6" h., 5 1/2" h., and 5 1/2" h. *Collection of Ernie & Bev Dieringer.*

Panelled Octagon child's teapot, sugar bowl, and creamer by Jacob Furnival. Teapot, 6" h.; sugar bowl, 5" h.; creamer, 3" h. *Collection of Ernie & Bev Dieringer.*

Lily of the Valley child's tea set by Anthony Shaw with Tea Leaf decoration. Note the handle-less tea cups. Teapot, 5 1/4" h. *Courtesy of Dale Abrams.*

Grape Octagon child's teapot, sugar bowl, and creamer. Teapot, 6 1/4" h. *Courtesy of Dan Overmeyer.*

Lily of the Valley white ironstone child's tea set by Anthony Shaw. Teapot, 5 1/2" h. *Courtesy of Dale Abrams.*

Floral Shape child's teapot, sugar, creamer, cup, and saucer by T. & R. Boote, 1852. Teapot, 6" h.;
sugar, 4 3/4" h.; creamer, 3" h.; cup, 2 1/4" h., 2 1/2" dia.; saucer, 4 1/4" dia. *Courtesy of Dan Overmeyer.*

Double Line Primary child's tea set in the Flow Blue *Lahore* pattern by
Thomas Philips & Son, ca. 1840. Teapot, 5 1/2" h. *Courtesy of Dan Overmeyer.*

Full Ribbed child's tea set by Pankhurst. Teapot, 6" h.; sugar bowl, 5" h.; creamer
3 1/8" h. to the lip; waste bowl, 3 3/4" dia., 2 1/2" h.; cup, 2" h. x 2 3/8" dia.;
saucer, 4 1/4" dia.; and plates, 4 1/4" dia. plates. *Courtesy of Dan Overmeyer.*

Child's Lily of the Valley Tea Leaf coffeepot with its adult-sized counterpart presents an interesting comparison. *Courtesy of Dale Abrams.*

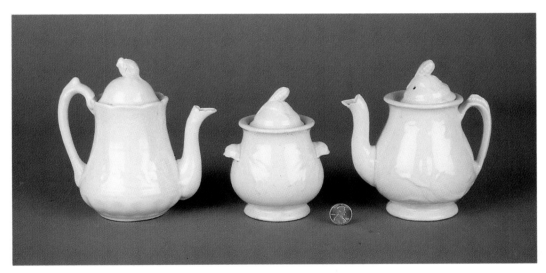

New York Shape child's teapot, 5 3/4" h. (left), shown with a Corn and Oats child's teapot and sugar, teapot, 5 3/4" h. (right). *Courtesy of Dan Overmeyer.*

Anthony Shaw's Lily of the Valley child's tea set in Tea Leaf, with handled cups. Teapot, 5 1/4" h. *Courtesy of Dale Abrams.*

Octagon shape child's tea set by T. & R. Boote, 1851. Left to right: tea pot, 6 1/2" h.; sugar bowl, 5 3/4" h.; waste bowl, 2 1/2" h. x 3 3/4" dia.; creamer, 3 1/4" h. *Collection of Ernie & Bev Dieringer.*

Panelled Grape child's teapot, sugar, and creamer attributed to Jacob Furnival shown with a set of child's stacking platters. Teapot, 6 1/2" h., sugar bowl, 5 1/4" h., creamer, 3 1/2" h. to lip, platters range from 3" to 5 1/8" wide. *Courtesy of Dan Overmeyer.*

Six-Panelled Trumpet child's tea set by J. W. Pankhurst. Teapot, 6" h. *Courtesy of Dan Overmeyer.*

Unknown shape child's teapot, sugar, and creamer by
Jacob Furnival. Teapot, 6" h. *Courtesy of Dan Overmeyer.*

Gold Lustre octagon child's dinner set, ca. 1840.
Large plates, 4" dia. *Courtesy of Lorraine Punchard.*

Ribbed child's tea set by J. & G. Meakin.
Teapot, 4 1/2" h. *Courtesy of Dan Overmeyer.*

Mulberry child's dinner set in *Chinese Bells* by Charles Meigh.
Large plate is 3 1/2" dia. *Courtesy of Lorraine Punchard.*

Child's teaset decorated in the Flow Blue *Scott's Bar* pattern.
Teapot, 4" h. *Courtesy of Gale Frederick and Dan Overmeyer.*

Another Mulberry dinner set by Charles Meigh, transfer deorations of hopberries
and vines, ca. 1835-1849. Soup tureen is 5" h. *Courtesy of Lorraine Puchard.*

A teapot, sugar bowl, cup and saucer from a Knowles, Taylor & Knowles American child's tea set in Tea Leaf. Teapot, 5 1/2" h.; cup, 2 1/4" h, 2 1/4" dia. *Courtesy of Dale Abrams.*

Unknown shape child's teapot, sugar bowl, and creamer. Teapot, 5" h.; sugar bowl, 4 1/2" h.; creamer, 3" h. to the lip. Note the bird's head on the spout. *Courtesy of Dan Overmeyer.*

Gold Lustre slant-sided child's set by Mellor, Taylor, & Co. Teapot, 6" h.; cup, 2 1/4" h. and 2 3/4" dia.; plate, 5" dia. *Courtesy of Dale Abrams.*

Gold Lustre bulbous child's set, also by Mellor, Taylor & Co. The cup, saucer, and plate shown here are the same as the slant-sided set. Teapot, 5 1/2" h. *Courtesy of Dale Abrams.*

A child's undertray, probably to a sauce tureen, 4" w. handle to handle. *Courtesy of Dan Overmeyer.*

Child's wash bowl and pitcher. Pitcher, 4" h., 4 1/2" dia. *Courtesy of Dan Overmeyer.*

Three sizes of Anthony Shaw children's mugs in Tea Leaf decoration. The largest is 3" h., 3" dia.; the smallest measures 2 1/2" h., 2 1/2" dia. *Courtesy of Dale Abrams.*

Child's compote in white ironstone and in the *Scinde* pattern in Flow Blue, attributed to Alcock. 3 1/2" dia., 2" h. *Courtesy of Margot Frederick and Dan Overmeyer.*

Child's dinner set decorated in the Flow Blue *Asiatic Birds* pattern, maker unknown. The soup tureen measures 5 1/4" h., 6 1/2" handle to handle. *Courtesy of Margot Frederick.*

Mulberry tea set by Dixon & Co., ca. 1822-1833. Teapot, 5 1/2" h. *Courtesy of Lorraine Punchard.*

A partial child's dinner set decorated in the Flow Blue Scinde pattern, ca. 1840. The platter measures 6" w. and the sauce tureen measures 4" h. *Courtesy of Margot Frederick.*

Bibliography

Barber, Edwin Atlee. *Pottery and Porcelain of the United States.* New York: Century House Americana, 1971.

Chaffers, William. *Marks & Monograms on European and Oriental Pottery and Porcelain.* London: William Reeves, 1965.

Cox, Warren. *Pottery & Porcelain.* New York: Crown Publishers, 1944.

Godden, Geoffrey A. *British Pottery and Porcelain 1780-1850.* New York: A. S. Barnes and Co., Inc., 1963.

_____. *Encyclopaedia of British Pottery and Porcelain Marks.* New York: Bonanza Books, 1964.

Heavilin, Annise Doring. *Grandma's Tea Leaf Ironstone.* Indiana: L-W Book Sales, 1981.

Hill, Ellen R. *Mulberry Ironstone: Flow Blue's Best Kept Little Secret.* New Jersey: Ellen Hill, 1993.

Hughes, Bernard and Therle. *The Collector's Encyclopaedia of English Ceramics.* London: Abbey Library, 1968.

Ramsay, John. *American Potters and Pottery.* New York: Tudor Publishing Co., 1947.

Snyder, Jeffrey B. *A Pocket Guide to Flow Blue.* Pennsylvania: Schiffer Publishing, Ltd., 1995.

_____. *Flow Blue: A Collector's Guide to Pattern, History, and Values.* Pennsylvania: Schiffer Publishing, Ltd., 1992.

_____. *Historic Flow Blue.* Pennsylvania: Schiffer Publishing, Ltd., 1994.

Upchurch, Nancy J. *Handbook of Tea Leaf Body Styles.* Tea Leaf Club International, 1995.

Wetherbee, Jean. *White Ironstone: A Collector's Guide.* Iowa: Antique Trader Books, 1996.

Punchard, Lorraine. *Playtime Pottery & Porcelain From the United Kingdom & the United States.* Pennsylvania: Schiffer Publishing, Ltd., 1996.

Value Guide

Values vary immensely according to the condition of the piece, the location of the market, and the overall quality of the design and manufacture. Condition is always of paramount importance in assigning a value. Prices in the Midwest differ from those in the West or East, and those at specialty antique shows will vary from those at general shows. And, of course, being at the right place at the right time can make all the difference.

All of these factors make it impossible to create an absolutely accurate price list, but we can offer a guide. The prices reflect what one could realistically expect to pay at retail or auction.

Note that all prices in this guide are based on the fact that the item being evaluated is in **mint condition**—with no discoloration, chips, cracks, hairlines, or significant crazing. Damaged pieces can be worth significantly less than the prices shown here.

The left hand number is the page number. The letters following it indicate the position of the photograph on the page: T=top, L=left, R=right, TL=top left, TR=top right, C=center, CL=center, CR=center right, B=bottom, BL=bottom left, BR=bottom right. Sequential numbers following immediately after these letters indicate the position of the piece in a series of pieces reading from left to right or top to bottom. The right hand column of numbers are the estimated price ranges in United States dollars. NMP=No Market Price available.

Page	Pos	Value
23	BL	25
24	TR	500+
	BL	140 Fig/Union, 110 Athens
	BR	215
25	CL	500-550
	CR	75-95
	BL	115
	BR	185-225
26	T	85-95
	CL	30-45
	CR	120-150
	B	200-245
27	CL	275-325
	B	600-800
28	TL	300+
	TR	300+
	BL	300+
	BR	55-125
29	TL	1000-1200
	CL	190 butter dish, 250 pancake server
	CR	450-575
	BL	250-300
	BR	35-45 plate, 75-85 cup plate, 65-75 sauce dish
30	TL	200-225
	BL	195-215
	BR	500-550
31	C	235-300
	B	195-250
32	TL	165-200
	TR	225-295 creamer, 125-165 sugar
	C	275-350
	B	175-250
33	T	NMP
	B	300+
34	T	125
	C	250-325 creamer, 300-375 milk pitcher
	BL	250+
	BR	250+
35	C	700+
	B	450+
36	TL	150+
	TR	450
	CR	45-55
	BL	35-50
	BR	300-375
37	T	350-400 coffeepot, 325-

Page	Pos	Value
		375 creamer, 250-300 sugar, 85-110 cup/saucer set
	C	125-150 coffeepot, 75-95 sugar, 75-95 creamer
	B	550-675 pitcher & bowl, 115 mug, chamber pot 350-475
38	TL	75-85
	TR	85, 65-70, 25-30, 35-45, 75-85
	C	750-900 sauce tureen, NMP soup tureen
	B	300-375 covered vegetable, 175-225 relish tray
39	TR	225-275
	C	L-R: 700+, 500+
	B	L-R: 85-135, 400-525, 175-250, 350-425
40	T	300-350
	C	300-350
	B	300-350
41	T	400-450
	C	750+
	B	1500-1700 set
42	T	1000+
	C	500+
	BL	300-350
	BR	250-300
43	T	325-400
	B	400-450
44	T	650
	C	400-450
	B	500+
45	T	290
	C	50
	B	300-350
46	T	1000-1200
	CL	750+
	CR	200-275
	B	250-300
47	T	500-550
	BR	125
48	TR	130
	C	210
	B	65-75
49	T	195-250
	BR	175-275
50	C	400-600
	BL	700+

Page	Pos	Value
	BR	450+
51	T	400
	BR	150-175
52	T	95-125 coffeepot, 85-110 teapot
	B	250-325 salt & pepper set, NMP plaque
53	TR	285-350 covered vegetable, 145-195 relish dish
	C	275-350
	B	300+
54	T	190
	C	60
	B	110
55	T	375-450
	BL	525-650 adult teapot, NMP child's teapot
	BR	525-650
56	T	475-650
	BL	395-425
	BR	165-185
57	T	65-95 sugar, 135-175 creamer
	CL	15-17 sauce dish, 12-15 butter pat
	CR	145-185
	B	425-495 with ladle
58	TL	175-225
	TR	75-85
	C	55-75
59	T	2000-2200
	C	500+
	B	1500-1700
60	T	700-1000
	C	700-750
	B	500+
61	C	1000+
62	T	110
	B	500+
63	TL	300-350
	TR	300-350
	BL	350-400
	BR	300-350
64	T	1200-1500 set
	C	350+
	BL	350-400
	BR	300-350
65	T	400-450
	B	L-R: 300+, 400+
66	TR	135-200

Page	Pos	Value
	C	100-135
	B	150-225 without insert
67	C	500+
	B	350+
68	T	200-250
	B	75
69	T	50
	C	275
70	TL	1500-1800+
	TR	525-575
	B	L-R: 135-175, 300-375, 95-125
71	T	500+
	BL	500+
	BR	350-400
72	T	L-R: 250-325 with ladle, 165-185, 300-375
	C	L-R: 325-400, 350-450
	B	500+
73	T	300-350
	B	125-150 each
74	T	35-50 small, 45-65 medium
	CL	300+
	BR	150
75	TL	375-450 pitcher, 75-85 sauce dish, 375-475 mug
	TR	425-525
	BL	75-85
	BR	375-475
76	TL	500+
	BR	NMP
77	TL	125-175
	CR	55
	BR	250+
78	T	500+
	BL	800-1000 set
	BR	300
79	TL	150-175 gravy boat, 275-350 pitcher
	TR	150
	CR	400-500
	B	325-375 creamers, 250-300 sugar bowls
80	T	350-425
	CL	195-250
	CR	425-475 each
	B	325-425
81	T	range from 275-400
	BL	25-35 plate, 65-75 cup plate

Page	Pos	Value / Description
	BR	750-100 soup tureen (2-pc., no ladle), 225-300 butter dish (3-pc.), 275-375 soap dish (3-pc)
82	TR	500+
	CR	195-265
	B	300-350
83	T	300-350
	C	300-350
	B	200-250 each
84	T	650-700
	B	NMP
85	T	375-475
	BL	350-375
	BR	750
86	TR	500+
	BR	500+
87	T	500+
	B	500+
88	T	400-450
	C	350-425 footed tureen (2-pc. no ladle), 175-225 coffeepot, 350-425 covered vegetable
	B	400-500
89	TL	325-400
	TR	200
	CL	225-325 sugar, 325-400 creamer
	CR	25-35 plate, 75-85 cup plate
	B	425-500
90	T	350-425 milk pitcher, 85-135 sugar, 350-425 milk pitcher
	BL	150-200
	BR	200-250
91	TR	150
	CR	225
	B	500+
92	T	135-185 coffeepot, 300-400 sugar bowl, 450-550 coffeepot
	C	30-40 each
	B	90
93	TL	425-525 coffeepot, 275-350 sugar bowl
	CL	175-225 Banded, 275-350 Tea Leaf
	CR	500+
94	T	500+
	BL	500-550
	BR	700+
95	C	1000-1500
96	T	200-235
	CL	375-475
	CR	295-395
	B	65-80
97	TL	200-225
	BR	185-250
98	TR	75-90
	BR	400-525 Reverse Teaberry, 375-425 Morning Glory
99	T	425-550 Teaberry coffeepot, NMP Coral sugar bowl, 150-175 Lustre Band creamer
	C	890
	BR	150
100	TR	700+
	C	1000-15000
	BL	500-550
	BR	500-550
101	T	500-550
	BL	3000+
	BR	700+
102	T	1000-1100
	CL	350-400
	CR	1000+
	B	700+
103	TL	700+
	TR	700+
	C	500-550
	B	1000-1100
104	T	NMP pitcher & bowl, 1100 creamer
	BL	500-550
	BR	800-1000
105	T	500-550 teapot, 200-250 creamer
	BL	175
	BR	700+
106	T	325-400 Pinwheel teapot, 150-195 covered butter (2-pc.), 135-200 coffeepot
	BL	140
107	TL	275-325 Tea Leaf, 150-175 Lustre Band
	C	75-100 waste bowl, 300-375 butter
108	TR	60
	BR	500-550
109	T	135
	CL	650
	CR	500+
110	T	500+
	BR	165-225
111	TL	95-150
	TR	30-45
	CR	500+
	BR	95-145
112	T	185-225
	C	NMP plaque, 175-225 sauce tureen (4-pc.)
113	T	200-250 each candlesticks, 60-85 cake plate
	B	125
114	T	95-145
	C	825
	B	1700-2000 set
115	T	175-225
	C	250-450
	B	125-175
116	T	100-175
	C	1500+
	B	700-1000
117	TL	700-1000
	TR	500+
	BL	300-350
	BR	350-500
118	T	275
	B	1500-2000
119	TL	225-275
	TR	350-375
	C	190
	B	300-500
120	TL	500+
	TR	500+
	C	75-100
	B	55
121	C	195
	B	500+
122	CL	135-200 sugar bowl, 145-200 creamer, 145-200 mug
	CR	500+
	B	375-475 3-pc. set
123	T	260-290 gravy boat, 470-520 covered vegetable
	C	1900-2100
	BL	200-250
	BR	400-450
124	CL	315
	CR	500+
	B	500-550
125	TL	500-550
	TR	600-650
	BL	400-450
	BR	500-600
126	TR	45-65
	B	135-200
127	T	450-600
	B	225
128	TL	375-450
	TR	50-100
	BR	50-100
129	C	500-550
	BL	NMP
	BR	150-195 pitcher, 95-110 cup/saucer set, 135-185 gravy boat
130	TL	125-185
	TR	150-195
	B	75-90
131	TL	125-165 creamer, 100-125 sugar bowl
	TR	45-55
	BL	75-90
	BR	35-50 pie plate, 85-125 salt & pepper set
132	T	300-400
	B	NMP
133	T	75-125
	B	300-400
134	T	300-400
	B	300-400
135	C	600-650
136	T	250-275
	B	40
137	T	400-600
	BL	140-150
	BR	400-500
138	T	250-450
	B	200+
139	T	400-500
	B	500-700
140	T	300+
	C	NMP
	B	75-100
141	T	200-300
	C	L-R: 2000, 700-1000
	B	700-1000
142	TL	500
	TR	700-1000
	B	700+
143	T	300-400
	C	L-R: 600-750, 500+
	B	700-1000
144	B	700-1000
145	T	400-450
	B	165-200
146	T	350-850
	BL	85-125
	BR	NMP
147	TL	175-200
	TR	250-300 egg cup, NMP small size egg cup, 300-350 wide mouth egg cup
	CL	250-300
	CR	150+
	B	NMP
148	TL	400-600
	TR	300+
	B	400-450
149	TL	400-600
	TR	400-600
	BL	400-500
	BR	400-500
150	T	500-700
	B	500+
151	T	L-R: 750, 500
	BL	NMP
	BR	300+
152	C	1200-1700+
153	TL	750-800
	TR	1500-1800
	BL	350-500
	BR	300-450
154	TL	350-500
	TR	500+
	B	1000+
155	T	800-1200+
	B	NMP
156	T	500+
	B	700+
157	TL	1500-2000
	TR	750+
	C	350-500
	BL	600-750
	BR	300-400+
158	T	450-500
	BL	500-550
	BR	300-450
159	T	650+
	CL	650+
	CR	700-850
	BL	500+
	BR	500-650
160	T	400-450
	B	400-450
161	TL	400-500
	TR	300-450
	C	2000-2200
	B	950-1050
162	T	2000-3000
	B	1800-2500
163	T	700+
	C	1000-1200+
	B	1000+
164	TL	500
	TR	500-800
	BL	150-175
	BR	400-450
165	T	2500+
	C	1000+
	B	1200-1500
166	T	1000+
	C	2200-2700
	B	1800-2200
167	T	400-500 adult, 550-600 child's
	C	300-500
	B	3000+
168	T	800-900 with six cups and saucers
	C	1000 teaset, 500-650 plate
	B	1500+
169	T	1000+
	C	800-1000
	B	2000-2500
170	T	800-1200
	C	1200-1500
	B	1800-2200
171	TL	100-135 teapot, 65-95 sugar bowl, 45-55 cup and saucer
	TR	700+
	C	1250-1750 complete set
	B	1250-1750 complete set
172	TL	200+
	TR	400-600
	C	350-450 each
	B	L-R: 800-1000, 300-400
173	T	2000+
	C	1400-1700
	B	3000+